# THE ELITE

## THINK LIKE AN ATHLETE, SUCCEED LIKE A CHAMPION

DR. JO LUKINS

JOHNATHAN THURSTON

Copyright © 2019 by Dr. Jo Lukins

All rights reserved.

ISBN

Paperback - 978-1-925884-36-4

Ebook - 978-1-925884-37-1

Dr Jo Lukins has asserted her right under the Copyright, Designs and Patents Act 1988 to be identified as the author of this work. The information in this book is based on the author's experiences and opinions. The publisher specifically disclaims responsibility for any adverse consequences, that may result from the use of the information contained herein. Permission to use information has been sought by the author. Any breaches will be rectified in further editions of the book.

All rights reserved. No part of this publication may be reproduced, stored in or introduced into a retrieval system, or transmitted in any form, or by any means (electronic, mechanical, photocopying, recording or otherwise) without the prior written permission of the author. Any person who does any unauthorised act in relation to this publication may be liable to criminal prosecution and civil claims for damages. Enquiries should be made through the publisher.

*Editor:* Marinda Wilkinson

*Publisher:* Elite Edge Publishing

# CONTENTS

| | |
|---|---|
| Thank you | v |
| Foreword | vii |
| 1. Take Your Mark | 1 |
| 2. Mindset Master Plan | 8 |
| 3. Success On Autopilot | 21 |
| 4. The Bannister Effect | 34 |
| 5. Systems In Place | 47 |
| 6. Tell It Straight | 55 |
| 7. Embrace The Suck | 65 |
| 8. Life Balance B.S. | 77 |
| 9. In Your Corner | 87 |
| 10. The Gratitude Attitude | 96 |
| 11. Enjoy The Ride | 104 |
| 12. So It Begins | 111 |
| The Elite Sleep Guide | 119 |
| Dr. Jo Speaker | 121 |
| About the Author | 123 |
| Your next read with Dr. Jo | 125 |
| Further Reading And References | 127 |
| Dr Jo & The Elite | 131 |

♥

To the athletes, professionals, teams and organisations who have entrusted and invited me into your lives - it is your stories, journeys, challenges and successes that have made this book possible. Thank you, I have learnt so much.

♥

To my family and friends, it takes a village for so many things: to raise a child, to face life's challenges and triumphs, and to write a book. It is exciting to take on a new project and it is made special when you do so with the unwavering support of those who believe in you. Thank you to my village – I promise there will be plenty of bubbles at the launch.

♥

There is no doubt for me who is 'in my corner'. To my husband Joe and sons Lachlan and Dylan - from the moment I first mentioned writing this book, you have been a foundation of love, support and encouragement. From the late-night conversations, the IT support and the 'How many words today, Mum?', you have championed me from start to finish. To the moon and back xxx

# FOREWORD
## BY JOHNATHAN THURSTON

The mental side of sport should never be underestimated. It isn't necessarily the best team or the most talented athletes who win, but those who understand that decision-making under pressure is critical to performance. Working on your mental game is as important as your physical targets and your competition strategy.

Dr. Jo Lukins is an expert in understanding athletes and professionals and helping them to be their best. In this book she shares her experience of over 25 years and links the secrets of success in sport to how you can achieve more.

My career in professional sport taught me that success comes from being physically fit, tactically skilled and mentally ready. Athletes understand the importance the mind plays in getting to the top of their game; the same principles can be applied in business and in life. This book provides a rare window into the mindset of those that excel in sport, sharing practical strategies you can implement now.

In addition to her experience with athletes, Jo is an academic and professional speaker. She is able to take the latest psychological research and translate it into 'how to's' for improving and succeeding.

Dr. Jo has an art for taking something complex and challenging you to think about it in a practical way that works.

Your mental approach can be your greatest asset or your biggest downfall. High performing athletes soon learn that you need to invest as much time on your mental approach as the physical part of your game to perform at your best. When times get tough, use your disappointments as motivation. We can all benefit from the lessons taught in our sporting arenas. We need someone that can translate the lessons and Dr. Jo has done that for us in this book. Learn the skills to think smarter, play smarter and be happier and you will always be the winner.

The most important message of this book is that we can all improve, achieve, be successful and happy. Dr. Jo doesn't promise that it's easy, but when you've experienced success, you will always know that it's been worth it! I am really glad that Dr. Jo has written this book and hope that you enjoy it as much as I did.

Johnathan Thurston

# CHAPTER 1
# TAKE YOUR MARK

> The expert at anything was once a beginner.
> Helen Hayes

> Hope is not a strategy, luck is not a factor, fear is not an option.
> James Cameron

AND IN A MOMENT, IT IS OVER. THE SIREN HAS GONE, THE whistle has blown, they have crossed the line or touched the wall. Hands shake, arms are raised in exhalation, tears are wept, smiles or frowns form and the contest is over.

It may seem strange to begin a book at the finish line, but for the elite performer, they know it is not the end. Rather, it's a point of transition where the performance cycle is about to roll through again. Prepare, train, compete, prepare, train, compete. Over and over the routine repeats. Each time the athlete either embraces the opportunity to become wiser, to grow and improve - otherwise, the moment is gone, and they'll line up to repeat the same mistakes again. Regardless of the sport, an astute athlete will always take the opportunity to reflect on their performance, to better understand the causes of their successes and failures. That way, they can plan to be better next time.

Michael Jordan hardly needs an introduction. Applauded for his skill, finesse, and ability to ' just do it', he is unarguably one of the greatest players to ever grace a basketball court. Yet perhaps his most important lesson was his ability to reject the negative, even from a very young age. When told he was not good enough to make the high school varsity basketball team, he used it as motivation to improve. Importantly, he very clearly understood that failure is not the opposite of success, but rather an integral part of it.

Those who have excelled in their sport have learnt (sometimes tough) lessons to reach their level of excellence. Roger Bannister, on the brink of retirement, asked a simple but profound question that would lead him to become the first person to run the mile in under four minutes. It was a question that other athletes of similar ability had not asked, and it was this possibility thinking that cemented him in the record books as the first person to run a mile under that elusive time.

Cathy Freeman ran on some of the greatest sporting stages, none bigger than the 400m at the Sydney Olympics in 2000. With the weight of her country's expectations on her shoulders, she stood tall and proud. With a strategy that had served her well throughout her athletic career she approached the line to run herself into sporting history.

I have spent my career researching and gaining understanding from outstanding athletes. Working with those who have risen to the top of their game, embraced opportunities and succeeded. Athletes who have encountered adversity, at times failed, then dusted themselves off and started again. Sport offers us a powerful metaphor for life. It's a place where we can witness inspiration, drama and success. There are many important lessons we can learn from elite athletes.

My hope for you in reading this book is that these insights will give you powerful new learnings and strategies that will help you elevate yourself from good to great. In sharing with you what I know to be part of their success, I hope to give you an insight into the thinking patterns and actions of those who have succeeded when others have failed and have excelled at the highest level. Through the 'wisdom of the elite' you will gain powerful understandings from those who have collectively toiled for years to uncover the key psychological strategies to stand amongst the best.

Sport is the toy store of life. Earl Warren once said, 'I always turn to the sports pages first, which records people's accomplishments. The front page has nothing but failures'. It's in the back pages of our papers we see the triumphs, the tears, the dreams and the heroes. Sadly, the front page is almost always overwhelmingly full of negativity. As humans we want good news, stories of success and achievement. Any wonder we seek to find inspiration from the world of sport and hope for it in our own lives. So here is the good news. There are teachings in the world of sport that we can transfer into our work, families and play. Whilst hope is not a strategy, it can certainly provide us with a great foundation for the lessons we can learn to be our best.

Success leaves clues, and sometimes those clues are right in front of us. The aim of this book is to share the knowledge and lessons that athletes have learnt to enhance their success. We can all benefit from these lessons. With some consideration, planning and implementation of the insights within this book, we can all learn to think like a champion.

Without a doubt the most precious commodity that each of us has is time. In the 24 hours we are gifted every day, we make decisions (sometimes consciously, sometimes on autopilot) as to how we want to spend that time. You hear people comment all the time about how busy they are, how things don't get done because they don't have enough time or how people feel rushed to get everything done.

Making time and prioritising yourself to achieve excellence is my challenge to you.

The truth is that you do have enough time, we all do. Part of the challenge is understanding that it's not because you're too busy but rather because it's not your priority. Choosing wisely how we spend our time is the key to our success. So, before we get too much further, I want you to be sure that your time will be well spent considering the lessons within this book and their application within your life.

## WHY YOU DON'T NEED TO READ THIS BOOK

I'm a big fan of transparency and while I would love to think that this book needs to be read by everyone, the reality is that it doesn't. If I were standing in a bookshop deciding what to take with me on my next plane trip or to inspire me in some aspect of my life, I want to be sure I make the right choice. So, here are some reasons why this book may not be for you:

Some people are completely happy and comfortable with their lives and are not interested in anything changing. And if that's you, that's fantastic. In fact, maybe it's you that should be writing a book!

If life is travelling well for you and you are satisfied with each aspect of your life (personal, work, relationships, health and sport) then keep doing what you're doing. Not everyone needs to make changes and your happiness and satisfaction is the best measure. Rather, this book is designed for those seeking to find an extra 5-10% on top of your existing success. If this isn't you, then save yourself some time. Gift this book to someone who can benefit from becoming better. And enjoy your flight.

## WHY YOU SHOULD READ THIS BOOK

It's most likely that in picking up this book you are someone who is motivated to be the best version of you, because you know you can be more than you currently are.

You are in the right place if:

You're succeeding well in aspects of your life and know that it would only take a few changes, strategies and actions on your part to be as successful as you can be.

You've already got some runs on the board, however you know you haven't yet reached the heights of your capabilities. If you would like to gain an insight into the way that elite performers operate and learn some of those strategies for yourself, then this is a book that can help.

With that in mind, here are some pointers that will help you take the information and turn it into something practical and beneficial.

## BUT DON'T I HAVE TO READ THE WHOLE BOOK?

Sure. That would be great. It would certainly be my recommendation! But as mentioned earlier, your time is exactly that, your time. Therefore, I have written the book so that the chapters standalone and can be read independently of each other. They are written in an order that makes sense to me, however, if you have particular priorities that you are really keen to get started on, you may wish to head straight there. If so, the below guidelines will help you decide which page to turn to first.

***Chapter 2:*** Because your attitude can be your biggest barrier. You want to be more positive and believe you can improve, you're just not sure how.

***Chapter 3:*** Because you know you'd be more successful if your self-control was better. Your habits need a tweak, or a complete overhaul. *A bonus tip:* If you read this and think 'Ugh, no thanks' – then this is your chapter. Possibly your most important chapter. Success is not about doing all the bright and shiny things - it comes from methodically doing what's needed every day. Understanding the key to winning habits is the pathway to success.

***Chapter 4:*** Because your life is feeling a little *vanilla*. When you're looking for a spark, the foundation of motivation is triggered through creativity. Finding new ways to excel and improve is your answer.

***Chapter 5:*** Because you want to be a winner and don't know the formula. You need the tools to sort out your system for success.

***Chapter 6:*** Because you need to get rid of the rubbish in your life and get what you really want. Holding up the mirror and being honest with yourself will help you to get real and get results.

***Chapter 7:*** Because you need to be able to push through and beyond when it gets tough. If you come away from events knowing that you could have done more and you didn't, this chapter will help.

***Chapter 8:*** You want it all and you don't know how. Spoiler alert – you can't have it all. And it gets worse, if you want to excel and you want *complete balance*, you are kidding yourself. That being said, you can still have a fulfilling life when striving for excellence. Read this chapter to find out how.

***Chapter 9:*** Because people matter. Your success is based on the people around you and those with whom you rely upon for support. How you manage your relationships with others is critical to your life, wellbeing and performance.

***Chapter 10:*** Because you want a life that's happier! Promise. Guaranteed. Whilst the *stuff* of life won't make you happy (well it will, but not for long), the contents of this chapter will bring you much closer to a genuine happiness.

***Chapter 11:*** Because with your 'eye on the prize' you don't want to miss the bigger picture. There is a balancing act between the journey and the outcome, and this chapter helps you to keep your eye on what matters.

**Chapter 12:** The final chapter brings together each of the key concepts of the book, to be sure you got each of the lessons and strategies and are ready to make changes moving forward.

## A FINAL WORD

Interestingly, as I was typing this chapter, the television was on in the background. A life coach was being interviewed and he was sharing details of the clients he had worked with, the work he had done and the successes he had brought to them.

That won't be happening here. Your success is 100% yours – I'm not interested in taking credit for your wins and achievements. Nor will I be responsible for those times when you put yourself on the line and don't get what you want. What I offer is knowledge and insights to the mental strengths of great athletes and teams. I will present these to you along with practical strategies that allows you to adapt them into your life whether it be in your sport, your work, or your family. Any successes you achieve are yours. I'll never go on television and brag that the reason you are successful is because of me, promise.

No longer is success only for an exclusive few; the greats of the game. The reality is success is possible for everyone. For this we do not need to lower the benchmark but rather see the possibility within ourselves. You can find the greatness in yourself, should you choose to look. You too can think and succeed like an elite athlete.

Let's get started.

# CHAPTER 2
# MINDSET MASTER PLAN

> If you put forth the effort, good things will be bestowed upon you.
> Michael Jordan

> If my mind can conceive it, and my heart can believe it – then I can achieve it.
> Muhammad Ali

THE OFFICIAL NATIONAL BASKETBALL ASSOCIATION (NBA) website describes Michael Jordan as the greatest basketball player of all time. Over 15 seasons in the NBA he played for both the Chicago Bulls and Washington Wizards. He holds the NBA record for a regular-season scoring average of 30.12 points per game and was involved in six championships through the course of his career. He is an athlete that requires little introduction and receives great adulation from those that played alongside and against him. When you consider the greatness of Jordan as an athlete, what percentage would you credit being due to his talent? 10%... 50%... 90%?

Jordan was undoubtedly an athletic superstar. But how does such sporting success develop? When we look through the lens of nature vs. nurture, to what extent are you born with talent, and how much is cultivated through effort and opportunity? Looking back over the career of the now mid 50-year-old, 'talented' would be an accurate descriptor of his ability. Yet a 'gifted athlete' is certainly not how Jordan would first have been described. As a high school player Jordan was judged to not be tall enough to make his varsity team. The coach was looking for someone around six foot seven, rather than Jordan's five foot ten. At this early stage, before his career had even begun Jordan was faced with the test that all athletes must endure at some point - rejection and disappointment. That sobering moment when you set out to achieve a goal, and failure results.

As painful as disappointment can be, those that achieve excellence soon understand that it is not the opposite to success, but rather a crucial part of it. When we experience failure, it is less about what happens to us, and more about how we respond to it that matters. Too often people walk away at the first point of rejection, when viewing it with an improved mindset could be the difference between long-term disappointment and success.

## WHY YOUR MINDSET MATTERS

Mindset has been extensively explored in psychological research. Professor Carol Dweck from Stanford University has devoted much of her career to understanding the way mindset affect performance. Fundamentally, your mindset is related to your beliefs around whether ability, intelligence and talent are genetically or environmentally determined.

Those with a fixed mindset believe their intelligence is set, and their capacity is not likely to change greatly. A fixed mindset is based on the assumption that talent is the greatest predictor of success and can't be changed. The fixed mindset will prevent you from even contemplating working on your bad habits or areas for growth because you are not open to the idea that they can be improved. A fixed mindset may result in you giving up prematurely on persevering with a difficult task.

Had Jordan held a fixed mindset he would most likely think he would always be too short and not good enough to make the team. A fixed mindset becomes stressful when encountering change, because perseverance is unlikely when we feel helpless in a situation. The self-talk or the excuse of 'it's just the way I am' gives us permission to quit.

In contrast, a growth mindset focuses on achieving improvement through effort, learning and persistence. Extending on the work by Dweck, within sport settings I refer to this as a *performance mindset*. A performance mindset is the foundation to believing you can improve at anything if you try and are mentally prepared for achievement. When you choose to view the world through a performance mindset, you are more likely to consider your potential rather than be limited by your current ability.

An indicator of Jordan's mindset is evident in one of his most famous quotes:

> I've missed more than 9000 shots in my career, I've lost almost 300 games. Twenty-six times I've been trusted to take the game winning shot and missed. I failed over and over again in my life and that is why I succeed.
> Michael Jordan

Here's a little exercise we'll use to get you thinking like Michael Jordan. Fill in the gaps and we'll revisit your responses later in the chapter.

*Think about an aspect of your life that is important to you and finish the below sentences with the first thing that comes into your mind.*

1. *I find it difficult to* _____

2. *I'm going to try to* _____

3. *If I* _____ *then* _____

4. *I can't* _____

## IS YOUR MINDSET HOLDING YOU BACK?

Sport provides athletes and coaches with opportunities to take risks. To set a goal and attempt to achieve it requires a willingness to be both vulnerable and resilient if it doesn't eventuate. Mindset is what defines your resilience - and your reaction will ultimately define your success.

A performance mindset is what enables you to take a disappointment and turn it into a learning experience. Most people think only of talent as the predictor of performance when it comes to sporting prowess, 'she's a natural' being a common statement. Observing someone who has been successful may make it appear as if it comes easily and with minimal hard work or effort. The truth is, the athlete who is highly talented is limited by that talent if they don't also apply effort and belief. Reaching the pinnacle of your sport, work, or any other pursuits will only come when you combine talent with effort and a helpful mindset.

Consider the following examples which illustrate the differences between fixed and performance mindset thinking.

## SPORT

> I'm just bad at it and I don't care (FIXED)

> It doesn't seem to be a priority for me right now (PERFORMANCE)

> I'm never going to be able to jump higher than 1.8m (FIXED)

> I haven't learnt how to jump that high, yet (PERFORMANCE)

> I'd really like to learn to serve well, but I just can't (FIXED)

> I'd really like to learn to serve well, I need to work at it (PERFORMANCE)

## WORK

> I never seem to be able to keep my diary organised (FIXED)

> In the past, when I tried to keep my diary organised, I didn't have much success (PERFORMANCE)

## RELATIONSHIPS

> You never listen to me (FIXED)

> There have been times when I have felt like you weren't listening to me (PERFORMANCE)

## LEARNING

> I'll never be good at learning a new language (FIXED)

> My progress has been slow learning a language (PERFORMANCE)

## HEALTH

> I've got no self-control with sweet foods (FIXED)

> It's been hard for me to stop when I've had something sweet (PERFORMANCE)

## MUSIC

> I'm not musical (FIXED)

> I've improved at piano than when I first started (PERFORMANCE)

Notice how in many cases, the fixed mindset phrasing is an interpretation and negative judgment, whereas the performance mindset phrasing is much more of an observation. Remarking on things you've observed or perceived doesn't limit you in the same way that judging yourself or your skills can.

## THE IMPACT OF MINDSET ON YOUR WORK, HEALTH AND STUDY

Mindset is evident in both individuals and organisations. The coach's curse is defined by the mantra, 'because that's how we've always done it'. An assumption that something should remain as it is and be unwilling to change has proven corrosive for innovation and opportunity for athletes and teams. If you won the championship last year, don't expect a repeat of the same formula will win it this year. Every other team will try to emulate you. You need to grow and change. Understandably the status quo is comfortable and predictable, but it won't allow for growth or improvement. If you keep doing what you have always done, why would you ever expect anything to change? At best it will stagnate at your current level of performance.

On the other hand, performance mindset is beneficial for the engagement and wellbeing of team members. Further, a performance mindset will lead to increased efficiencies, an improved economic bottom line and better outcomes. In workplaces, those who report a performance mindset are more likely to view their colleagues as trustworthy and be engaged with their work and the company. They also believe it is safe to take risks at work and feel that innovation is fostered and encouraged.

In addition to its effects on progress and growth, a fixed mindset is linked with negative impacts on mental health. There is a body of research to suggest that a fixed mindset markedly impacts your experience of depression. Whilst your mindset may not necessarily protect you from depression, what it seems to do is influence how you respond to experiencing it. A person with a performance mindset who experiences depression is more likely to consider the challenges they are facing with flexibility of thinking. They are also more likely to stay engaged with their lives and become more determined to do something to improve their circumstances than those with a fixed mindset. Therefore, a performance mindset becomes a helpful lens through which to view distress and struggle.

A performance mindset can also foster achievement. An important study conducted by Prof. Dweck challenged capable math students in a high school setting. The students had completed and succeeded at a complex mathematics problem as part of the research. The students were then offered the opportunity to complete another problem either at the same level of difficulty as the previous, or one that was to be more challenging. The decision made by the students was reflective of their approach to mindset. Those with a fixed mindset more often chose the task with the same degree of difficulty. In contrast, those with a performance mindset preferred to tackle the more challenging task.

> This is a wonderful feature of the growth mindset. You don't have to think you're already great at something to want to do it and enjoy doing it.
> Carol Dweck

The importance of this finding in achievement is clear. When your mindset believes in the possibility of improvement and growth, you are more willing to take risks. Further, you are more likely to trust your ability to cope if you are unsuccessful. Students with a performance mindset saw the learning potential in the exercise and were less focused on the importance of the outcome. A fixed mindset makes challenges, even in ones where you demonstrate competence, stressful. A fixed mindset makes success a target to be attained and 'failure' an outcome to be avoided (and feared).

Repeatedly, the benefit of holding a performance mindset is evident. When you can see the opportunity to improve, grow and learn, you are more likely to achieve with engagement. In addition, when you view the world through the perspective of growth, you handle disappointment and failure better. A performance mindset will help you in many ways – in study, work, sport, health and in your relationships.

A fixed mindset increases anxiety and stress about failure. You will limit your opportunities and risk taking according to what you consider your capabilities to be. Even in situations where you are skilled and competent, you are likely to experience an increased fear of failure. If you have a fixed mindset you will not reach your potential. Your very own thinking will sabotage you and limit your success.

So, let me ask you – how much talent do you have? A bit? Lots? Buckets of it? Alternatively, how much of a contribution does practice, training, effort, experience and skill development contribute to your success? How you answer this says a great deal about your mindset.

## IS YOUR THINKING BASED ON A FIXED OR PERFORMANCE MINDSET?

**What is your mindset? Take this quick quiz to find out.**

1. I believe that talent is something you are born with and you either have it or you don't.    TRUE    FALSE
2. The chance to show others your ability is a key source of your motivation.    TRUE    FALSE
3. When you are talented, things will come more easily to you.    TRUE    FALSE
4. It is better to do the things you are successful at than to appear less talented.    TRUE    FALSE
5. When you don't achieve in something, it confirms there are some things that you just simply won't be good at.    TRUE    FALSE
6. I give my attention to the things I am good at and don't want to focus on negative feedback.    TRUE    FALSE
7. Sometimes things just don't work out and that is not your fault.    TRUE    FALSE

SCORING (add all scores): TRUE = 0    FALSE = 1

Your score will rate between 0 and 7. The higher you score the more you think with a performance mindset, which will maximise your potential. The lower you score, the greater the likelihood that you will plateau early and under achieve.

There's a good chance that if you've scored lower, you will react with a fixed mindset and be concerned you have 'failed' this test. No! This isn't a test to pass or fail, but rather an indicator of where your thinking is at now. Just by knowing there are alternative ways of thinking, you open up the possibility for change, which can then help you to achieve things you previously didn't think possible.

The key understanding of a performance mindset is that every training session, work meeting, and time spent on a project, is an opportunity to learn, execute strategy and evaluate your performance.

## DEVELOPING YOUR MINDSET

So, a reasonable question would be, is your mindset genetic or is it something that we learn? For this I must declare myself a fence-sitter. Not because I'm undecided, but because there is research supportive of the contribution of genetics and socialisation (how we have been raised) in terms of understanding the creation of our mindset. The important thing to know is that your mindset is something that can change and be developed. You can improve your mindset, and as a result get better outcomes and be happier with your achievements.

Remember the exercise you were asked to complete earlier in the chapter? Look back and have a read through your responses.

Perhaps it looked like this:
1. *I find it difficult to resist junk food in the afternoon.*
2. *I'm going to try to exercise every day.*
3. *If I take my multivitamins then I'll feel healthier.*
4. *I can't get up early in the morning.*

Read through each of the examples above and consider how they would make you feel if they were your statements. Now let's see what happens when we change the wording of the sentences.

1. *I find it ~~difficult~~ **a challenge** to resist junk food in the afternoon.*

As you can see from above, the language we use is instrumental in influencing how we feel. The difference (in number one) of taking on a challenge versus doing something difficult greatly alters how we feel about doing the task.

Many years ago, I worked with a professional rugby league player who completed the same written exercise. At the time he was the youngest person in the team and couldn't believe that he was in a team alongside some of the childhood heroes he had watched play on television. When he completed the sheet his response to number one was 'I find it difficult to speak in team meetings'. He admitted he found the room intimidating and he didn't want to risk saying something foolish in front of his teammates. This was despite often having an opinion, only to hear someone else say what he was thinking! Changing the first sentence had a profound effect upon his outlook. His sentence had now become, 'I find it a challenge to speak in team meetings'. Instantly his body language changed. He sat up taller, he smiled slightly and nodded. 'I like challenges,' he said.

The next week he returned to my office. When asked how his previous week had been, he smiled and said, 'It was good. I spoke in one of the meetings'. Thankfully his contribution had gone well, and the coach praised him afterwards for speaking up for the first time. 'You know Jo, I'm never going to have another problem again for the rest of my life,' he told me. A bold statement indeed. He concluded, 'From now on, no more difficulties - just challenges'. The benefits of a performance mindset – a life free from difficulties!

2. *I'm going to ~~try to~~ exercise every day.*
3. *~~If~~ **When** I take my multivitamin, **then** I'll feel healthier.*

In numbers two and three, changing the language from tentative and non-committal to strong and definite makes the outcome much more likely. When we consider things with ambiguous language, we are less likely to follow through. I have witnessed so many people make the slight shift in language from tentative to strong with great results. Hearing yourself make a verbal commitment is both motivating and obligating. Definite language becomes our call to action.

3. I ~~can't~~ ***won't*** *get up early in the morning.*

Finally, in number four, 'can't' language essentially places a barrier around us, making it unlikely that we'll ever achieve it. Whilst there are some true 'I can'ts' in the world, such as, I can't fly and I can't run 100m in seven seconds, many of the I can't sentences we say are simply a case of something we will not do, rather than can not do.

Example four is a good illustration of this. Anyone can get up early in the morning. Not everyone likes to. Not everyone chooses to. The key way to approach telling yourself that you won't do something is to consider the consequences of that choice. If you won't get up early, does it matter to the rest of your day? If not, enjoy your sleep in. If it does, then reconsider your choice.

When you hear yourself declaring that you can't do something, test it. Follow up with the question, 'Is that actually true?'. When you know the difference between your true limitations and your choices you can make better decisions. The language you use is fundamental to whether you view the world in a fixed or performance-based way. How you think matters and by challenging yourself to think more from a performance mindset, you set yourself up for success.

Research and academic environments are very clear that the performance of students can be clearly manipulated according to their exposure to performance versus fixed mindset set thinking. In one study a decline in maths scores of students was reversed simply by coaching the students in developing a performance mindset.

The brain works like a muscle. It will grow through effort, determination and practice. When you understand that your approach to your mindset is the gateway to reaching your potential, you are well on your way to success.

## HOW CAN YOU DEVELOP A PERFORMANCE MINDSET?

★ Insert 'yet' at the end of any sentences where you tell yourself that your ability is lacking.

★ Listen out for 'can't'. Is it true or are you telling yourself a convenient lie?

★ Focus on your effort. It's a more accurate judge of success and improvement than whether you won or lost.

★ Pick moments in your day to reflect on what you have learnt, how you're now different, what has changed and why you are better for the experience.

★ Consider adversity and setbacks. Set up your own 'post-performance review', to assess your performance, learn and plan forward for your growth and improvement.

# CHAPTER 3
# SUCCESS ON AUTOPILOT

> We first make our habits, and then our habits make us.
> John Dryden

> Quality is not an act; it is a habit.
> Aristotle

WITH THE EYES OF THE WORLD UPON HER, CATHY FREEMAN convinced the butterflies to fly in formation, and went on to win one of the greatest races in Australian sporting history.

At a little after 8pm on 25 September 2000 all eyes turned to the start of the women's 400m and the presence of Australian sprinter, Catherine Astrid Salone Freeman (our beloved Cathy). After months of being the most discussed Australian athlete, with the nation's highest expectations on her shoulders, she moved to lane six.

In an interview with Mark Howard, Cathy described the walk to the start line like this: 'You feel like you're a lamb going off to slaughter... I felt scared. Not scared where everything's falling apart – it's a feeling of, this is it, there's no turning back.' Her walk to the starting blocks had her focus solely on controlling her emotions so that she would have enough reserves to draw on in the final 150m.

Do you have a strategy that you can draw on every time you are on the brink of something exciting and the nerves kick in?

Having not been beaten in over two years, she placed her tracksuit in her crate and moved into position. Staring down her lane, the others on the track faded to grey. With a slow, deliberate exhalation she stepped forward with purpose to the front of the blocks. Resplendent in her green, gold and silver body suit she was an image of confidence and composure. Moving down into position, she carefully placed her fingers to the line, rocked from side to side twice and lowered her right knee to the track. With her head lowered, she was in the hands of the starter.

In the 40 seconds or so it takes an Olympic sprinter to set themselves into position, over 100 decisions have been made. With the strategy of the race to implement, the athlete who is better able to automate these processes, has more mental space available to focus on getting the job done. Cathy Freeman was able to channel her mental processing into the strategy of her race because she completed all the earlier, necessary behaviours on autopilot. When we have a habit, we have an automatic behaviour that frees our thinking to focus on the more important tasks.

## HABITS, AND WHY GOOD INTENTIONS ALONE ARE NOT ENOUGH

There is no doubt the people have great intentions. Sadly however, good intentions seem to have a bad reputation! The best time to listen for good intentions is on 31 December, usually around 8pm. Listen to those around you talk about what the following year is going to look like: becoming fitter, stronger, making more money, losing that last 10 kg or getting the job they have always wanted. If only it was this simple. Fitness app Strava recorded over 100 million activities in

2018. Their data shows that efforts significantly drop from 17 January each year. When you fast forward the clock from New Year's Eve to the third week of January most people have either not successfully put their goals into action or have discarded them entirely.

 The road to hell is paved with good intentions.
Henry G. Bohn

Sadly, the lessons from New Year's Eve is that good intentions are not enough for people to change their behaviour. Nor would it seem is knowledge. Whilst there are some who get caught up in myths or incorrect information regarding health and physical activity, most people have a good idea of what is needed to live a healthy life. Most understand that to stay hydrated, exercise, eat well, brush your teeth, get enough sleep and reduce time on your mobile devices is beneficial.

Spend a moment now to think about the behaviours you're currently not doing that you 'should be'. In many cases, simply knowing something is good for you isn't enough to compel you to actually do it. The key reason we don't do what we need to do is because we think it is hard. Most people will pick the easy decision over the hard decision, every time.

## HOW DO YOU MAKE YOUR DECISIONS?

How you make decisions and the information you pay attention to is the difference between the good and the excellent.

By the time you sip on your first morning coffee, you are likely to have already made more than 1,000 decisions. In fact, by the end of the day, it is estimated that most adults have made around 35,000 conscious decisions. Whilst that reads a large number, research from Cornell University determine people average 226.7 decisions per day on food alone! As your level of responsibility in life increases, so to do the multitude of choices that you make. Children only make an average of 3,000 decisions each day. For adults, whether it be deciding what to eat, what to wear, decisions at work, and whether to keep flicking through the TV channels or go to bed, it's no wonder we feel exhausted by day's end!

With so many decisions to be made each day, our brain has a clever way of reducing the load. Compacting behaviours into sequences we repeat every day – otherwise known as our habits. Would it surprise you to know that about 40% of what we do every day is habit? That does sound a high percentage - and it is – but remember back to this morning. Think about what you did within the first hour of getting up and the order in which you did it. Shower, get changed, turn on the TV, breakfast, prepare lunch, brush your teeth, get ready to leave for work/school. Perhaps that describes your morning fairly accurately, or maybe it included other activities such as exercise or household chores. Regardless, for most people reading this book the sequence of your morning is likely to be very similar day after day. Even down to the finer detail – the bowl you have your cereal in, where you sit for your morning cup of tea, the sequence of actions in your morning hygiene routine.

Life is too full to spend time considering whether you will hold your toothbrush in your left or right hand or the direction in which you will squeeze the paste. Our brain creates habits, an evolutionary life hack removing much of the decision making for us. Our habits are a substantial part of our everyday, so it's important that we utilise them to our best advantage.

The truth about habits – they are great, because they save us from having to think. The truth about habits - they are terrible, because they save us from having to think. You create your habits, and then your habits will control your life.

 The chains of habit are too weak to be felt until they are too strong to be broken.
Samuel Johnson

## DO THE HABITS YOU'VE BUILT INTO YOUR LIFE SERVE YOU WELL?

When Cathy Freeman lined up at the start of the 400m, she didn't have to repeat a memorised list of steps as to how best to get in the 'set' position. She did it on autopilot, because it was a habit. It was a habit because she had repeated that action in exactly the same way, over and over again. By acting on autopilot at the blocks her mind was fresh and free to think about the more complex aspects of the race. The same will work for you. Habits do the thinking for you, they give you less to think about rather than more to think about. When you have habits that work well for you, you have more brainpower available to devote to the complex stuff.

If your habits include daily physical activity, drinking plenty of water, getting enough sleep and reducing your time on social media then those habits are serving you well. In contrast, if you're staying up every night bingeing on too much TV, eating junk just before bed and spending most of your surplus cash on products from the infomercials, then those habits may not be serving you well. All our habits have consequences and it is beneficial for us to consider how helpful they are in reaching our end goal.

When used well, habits become your tool for streamlining your life. When you actively include the habits that will contribute to your success, your thinking will become clearer and you have more space in your head to make better decisions.

Ask yourself: how would your life benefit from new habits? Are there certain things you could introduce to your life that would serve you well, or are there existing habits that could be done better?

## THE ORIGINS OF YOUR HABITS

The starting point is to understand how habits are formed. Before becoming a habit, a behaviour must be identified as something that you wish to include in your life. Let's take the safety behaviour of wearing a seatbelt. As an infant and young child, the action of wearing a seatbelt is controlled by adults. Some children may fight the constraint of wearing their belt, but over time, they learn that the act of getting into a car and putting on a seatbelt go together. Over the years this pattern continues until we find ourselves as adults giving little or no thought to putting on a seatbelt, yet we do it automatically anyway. This is due to a phenomenon that humans respond well to – contingency behaviours.

Contingencies are the link for the before and after behaviours that create habits. Sitting in a car seat and putting on a seatbelt are behaviours that become automatically linked. Think about some of the other behaviours that you do that have a before and after consequence. Perhaps you go outside and put on sunglasses. Maybe you walk into the gym and go straight to the warm up area. Or, when you stand up to leave work, you straighten up your desk and push in your chair. These are all behaviours that you do, seemingly with little or no thought. Elite athletes also have contingency behaviours in place: finish a training session and drink a protein shake; eat dinner, then get on the foam roller; stand at the free throw line and bounce the ball three times before taking the shot. Whether the behaviours are functional or superstitious, contingencies are the glue for the automatic behaviours that athletes follow.

## THE POWER OF WHEN AND THEN

Now that you understand how contingencies work, it is useful to consider how to create new habits. For this we need to turn our focus to research conducted in Germany by social psychologist Peter Gollwitzer in 1997. Students were recruited to write an essay on their end of year break and post it within 48 hours of Christmas Day. Half of the students were given the additional task to write down when and where they would write the essay. For example, 'When it is Christmas afternoon, then I'll sit on the back verandah and write my essay'. Did this additional task make much difference to the response rate? Yes, it did.

The return rate for students who wrote down their 'when' and 'then' was 71% compared with just 32% for those who didn't. The difference was more than double. Is that right? Could that one small additional action really make that much of a difference? Yes, because the action feeds right in to the fundamental human response to contingencies. If you want to bridge the gap between a good intention and action the research is clear – set a when/then plan. By finding an opportunity in advance and pairing the behaviour that will go with it, you increase the likelihood of behaviour change by two to three times.

Incredibly, the same result has been consistently noted with many other behaviours, such as sticking with an exercise program, taking multivitamins, reducing gambling behaviour, breast self-examination, improving sleeping habits and studying for tests. The bottom line is that when you pair a new behaviour with an existing prompt you significantly increase the likelihood of changing the action.

The beauty of this simple strategy is that you can apply it to any behavioural goal. For example:

Goal: Not order dessert when at restaurants.
*When* the menu comes, *then* I'll order coffee.

Goal: Study an extra two hours a week.
*When* it's Monday night and I've cleaned the kitchen, *then* I'll sit at my desk and study until 9pm.

Goal: To get up when the alarm goes off, rather than hit snooze.
*When* the alarm goes off, *then* I get up.

For any of these goals, the conscious effort of linking the trigger (the 'when') and applying it to the new behaviour (the 'then') more than doubles the likelihood of you engaging in the behaviour.

## SOMETIMES IT'S THE LITTLE THINGS

I work with the Australian Defence Force and deliver sessions within a six-week resilience program. One of the groups were discussing the tyranny of alarm clocks, particularly the temptation of hitting the snooze button. I shared with the group that some people find it helpful to use a when/then strategy and set the alarm clock to go to bed. The alarm is a useful interruption when you're lying on the couch sucked into binge watching a series on Netflix. It might go something like, 'When the alarm goes off, then I start to get ready for bed'. By the end of the six weeks one officer said it had completely transformed his life. He mentioned the flow-on effects from going to bed in accordance with the alarm meant that he was regularly going to bed 90 minutes earlier than usual. This resulted in him

naturally waking an hour earlier each morning (no more morning alarm). The earlier rising meant that he was taking his dog for a 40-minute walk and then coming home and preparing his lunch for the day (he had previously been buying lunch at work). He was therefore eating healthier lunches and saving money, which he put towards an upcoming holiday. By changing one small behaviour he made a substantial change across his daily life.

> *Creating one small habit can ripple through your life like a stone thrown into a pond.*

To further clarify the strategy, let's consider it through an example most of us can relate to. We'll start with a question: when did you last floss your teeth? I thought so! Right now, most people reading this section are running their tongue over their teeth, because the percentage of the population who floss their teeth according to the recommendations made by dentists are less than 20%.

Flossing is another good example of a behaviour where knowledge is not enough to trigger action. When you don't floss, more than half the surface area of your teeth remain unclean. Flossing is also understood to prevent gum disease, tooth decay and bad breath. Dentists will tell you that most people only floss as recommended in the few days before they come in for their checkups – but this is clearly not enough.

One day, sitting with my hygienist and apologising for not regularly flossing (again) I realised that the when/then strategy might be perfect for getting me into the habit of regularly flossing. The challenge was to think of a behaviour that I did regularly that I might be able to pair with flossing. It feels foolish to admit how many years it took me to see the connection between brushing and flossing!

So, my new-found strategy sounded something like this:

Goal: To regularly floss.
*When* I'm holding a toothbrush, *then* I'll reach for the dental floss.

Certainly not rocket science, but wouldn't you know it – it worked! I can now proudly include twice-daily flossing as one of the helpful habits I do every day. Flossing your teeth may not initially seem like a huge behavioural change, although I can report that my dentist was delighted.

Importantly, with behaviour change and habits, a good way to kick things off is to start small. The research is also supportive of the contagious effects of behaviour change when we start with something that seemingly won't make a big difference. A famous speech delivered by US Navy Admiral William H. McCraven reminded the graduates of the importance to get up every morning and make your bed. He argued, 'If you can't do the little things right, you'll never be able to do the big things right'. Making your bed, flossing your teeth, putting things away – all little things, all make a difference.

## HELPFUL HABITS ARE CATCHING

The reason the little things make a difference is that like mood, habits are contagious. When you do one small thing well and you notice you have done it, your body rewards you with a small hit of dopamine. Dopamine is a neurotransmitter that is central to the motivational component of rewarding and motivating behaviour. In sport we talk about success being reached when we can conquer the one percenters. The athlete who takes the extra ball shots after training, does their stretching, records their data, drinks another bottle of electrolytes. All these seemingly small behaviours (the one percenters) reward motivation and reward discipline. And it is the disciplined athletes who are set up for success.

The take home message for you is that finding small habits within your life and implementing them through the when/then strategy will put you on the path to success. Whether it be picking up dirty socks, throwing out takeaway cups from your car, tucking in your chair or receiving an email and only handling it once. All these small practices, and helpful habits will make it easier for you to take on the bigger tasks. Athletes do this, and you can do it too. There is no point in tackling the big goals, until you have the smaller ones ticked off.

When you do these little things and conquer the small habits that make a difference in your life, please take note of what you are doing. When you are mindful that you are making a great choice for you, that effect is powerful. Noticing when you do things well is a moment of self-congratulation that you share with yourself. When you can momentarily look back on parts of your day and realise the helpful habits you put into place, it brings about a feeling of pride and satisfaction.

I never expect an elite athlete to pull out an important psychological skill on grand final day without them having practised it over and over in training and other game opportunities. In the high-pressure moments of life, you need the habits that will free up your thinking and set you up for success. Cathy Freeman developed those skills over hours, days and years of training. The habits of walking from warm up to the start and pacing herself through her run are habits in motion. Elite athletes understand that it is the small habits that you create that will result in your success.

You too can set up habits for success through the when/then strategy.

## BUT ISN'T IT ABOUT WILLPOWER?

I often hear people say, they wish they had greater self-control or more willpower. The ability to resist an unwanted behaviour such as a pie for lunch or hitting snooze three times in the morning rather than get up. The more helpful habits you have in place, the less you need to draw on willpower to make preferred choices. Willpower is a resource that we often tell ourselves is limited, that once we have exhausted our supply for the day, then we are much more vulnerable to unhelpful habits. I think one of the toughest challenges we face every day is moving our feet from mattress to floor. I'm a strong believer that once we can do that the greatest hurdle of the day is already achieved!

> *You are not always motivated... so you need to learn discipline. You will not always be disciplined... so you need to develop habits.*

## IS THERE A DOWNSIDE TO HABITS?

There is a word of caution with regards to habits. The advantage of habits is they require less thought and less attention to complete. However, it's not always the preferred option to be on autopilot. Let's consider your morning cup of coffee. If it's an everyday occurrence for you and is part of your habit routine, you may pour it and drink it without really noticing or enjoying it. So, be aware of what becomes automatic. If coffee is pleasurable for you, make sure you remain mindful enough whilst you're doing it that it doesn't pass you by without thought. For me, I've made a habit of tuning in to my morning coffee. In contrast, I'm happy for my flossing to become a less aware experience.

## ARE YOU SAYING I NEED GOOD HABITS?

The other thing you will note through this chapter is I don't refer to habits as being good or bad. I'm strongly of the opinion that it's unhelpful to label habits as good or bad. The simple reason being that if you label a habit as bad, and then do it, the only resulting emotion is a feeling of guilt. Instead, I would rather think about habits as moving along a continuum from less to more helpful. Life is challenging enough without loading yourself up with guilt for what you do or don't do. Consider the options in terms of the helpful and less helpful habits and then make your choices from there.

As you can see, it's possible to put your preferred behaviours on autopilot by creating helpful habits. Your habits reduce the number of decisions you need to make thus saving you the unnecessary drain on willpower. This increases your ability to set yourself up for success by undertaking the behaviours consistent with success.

## HOW CAN YOU CREATE HELPFUL HABITS IN YOUR LIFE?

★ Identify a target behaviour and pick a small habit to change (e.g. lowering the toilet seat, pausing before responding, making eye contact, listening well or tracking cash flow).

★ Consider why you haven't already been doing this behaviour.

★ Ask yourself why you are now ready to change.

★ Articulate the when/then.

★ Write down your when/then behaviour.

★ Monitor your progress.

Start building better habits today with a 30-day worksheet and video. Visit drjolukins.com/30-day-habit-streak

# CHAPTER 4
# THE BANNISTER EFFECT

> Sport, like all of life, is about taking your chances.
> Roger Bannister

> I'd like to see it as a metaphor not only for sport, but for life and seeking challenges.
> Roger Bannister

MOST OF THE WORLD THOUGHT IT IMPOSSIBLE WHEN ROGER Bannister claimed he could break the four-minute mile before he proved them wrong in 1954. Even Bannister himself almost quit. In the 1950's the thought of running a mile and completing it in under four minutes was not only considered to be humanly impossible, but death from the exertion required was speculated as a real possibility. The human body it was believed, was not designed to cope with such stress.

Would you take on a physical challenge where it's very attempt might result in your death?

In 1952 Englishman, Roger Bannister competed in the 1500m at the Olympic Games in Helsinki. In a hard-fought race and the placings decided in the final metres, he crossed the line in fourth place. Despite setting a British record with his result, he received considerable criticism of his placing. In the eyes of many he had underperformed. The result caused Bannister to consider his future in the sport, with the thought that he would retire from running. A re-evaluation of his distance and the setting of new goals refocused his target to running the mile in under four minutes.

Bannister was certainly not the first to attempt the four-minute mile record, in fact there are stories of runners pursuing this goal since the late 1800s. Considered for years as something of a 'Holy Grail' of sport the challenge was as much a psychological barrier as a physical one. The experts of the time speculated that on a hard, dry clay track in front of a noisy crowd would be the optimal conditions in which to make the attempt. Were they right?

On the morning of the run, Bannister followed his normal routine – attending work as a medical student at St Mary's Hospital. After working through his 40-patient ward, he spent time at the laboratory grindstone sharpening his spikes. That evening in May 1954 he travelled across to Oxford University and set out to break the record. Roger Bannister was criticised by the press for taking an unconventional approach. His different methods for training and preparation were a constant source of condemnation. However, he never wavered in his routine and self-belief. Unlike the optimal conditions described, the day was cold, the track was wet, and the crowd was only a few thousand people. Accompanied by pacers, Christopher Chataway and Chris Brasher, Bannister completed four laps of the track in 3:59:04 – a human performance that few had believed possible.

His hope was that his achievement would be seen by others as a symbol for overcoming adversity. Two months later, John Landy ran 3:58 minutes and the two would go on to race each other in what would be known as the Miracle Mile, with both breaking the four-minute benchmark.

The Miracle Mile race offers a further reminder, to never look back and to focus on your own game. Leading the race with only metres to go, Landy glanced back over his left shoulder to see the positioning of Bannister, only for Bannister to strategically pass him on his right and win the race. There's a clear lesson here - keep your eye on the prize, trust yourself and finish strongly.

## ARE YOU A BOUNDARY PUSHER?

There are so many elements of Bannister's story for us to draw upon. His self-belief, grit, tenacity and ability to face the adversity of a below standard performance in Helsinki enabled him to turn it around and complete one of the greatest sporting achievements in living history. Not only did he break a physical barrier on that day, but importantly a mindset one. He paved the way for others to believe it possible too - in the year that followed, 33 people broke the four-minute barrier.

The current record for the four-minute mile is 3:43:13. The thought that anyone would run that fast was inconceivable in the 1950's, an impossible feat. The challenge for each of us isn't necessarily to crystal ball what is possible, or to limit ourselves of our potential, but to consider how we might creatively consider new learnings, commitment and questions.

What boundaries will you choose to push in your life?

## ASK THE RIGHT QUESTION AND ANYTHING CAN HAPPEN

The pivotal moment for Roger Bannister's success was when he asked himself the question, 'What if a human can run that fast?'. This was the one defining moment that changed the trajectory of his success. The moment you commit to setting a unique goal is triggered at the point when the mindset question is asked. Roger Bannister did what the world thought unachievable, because he was able to ask himself that question. He viewed running and human performance in new ways and became a trailblazer, because he was willing to pursue and commit to a goal even when others viewed it with unbelievable doubt. Refusing to dwell in the negative mindset of others or accept unhelpful opinions, Bannister trusted his own methods in his preparation for the world record attempt. Increasing creative thinking in your life will be a great asset to your motivation and will assist you to build new pathways to success.

> The stupidity of people comes from having an answer for everything. The wisdom of the novel comes from having a question for everything.
> Milan Kundera

A well-considered question can generate a whole new field of possibilities and can prompt changes in entrenched habitual thinking. Your athletic intelligence is reflected in your ability to ask a wise and empowering question. Bannister first asked himself, 'What if I can run that fast?' followed by the question, 'What then must I do to make it happen?'. The answers to those questions saw his achievements permanently etched into the history books and he has left a legacy for all athletes to push the boundaries of what the world thinks is possible.

## SUCCESS STARTS WITH CREATIVE THINKING

Creative, possibility thinking is important for all levels of success. Take organisations who continue to prioritise creativity and possibility thinking within their culture. Apple and Dominoes are examples of companies who have found new ways to adapt, innovate and grow within their changing environment. In 1889, Punch Magazine described a conversation between a genius and a child. The genius asked, 'Isn't there a clerk who can examine patents?' to which the child replies, 'Quite unnecessary, Sir. Everything that can be invented has been invented'. That quote has since been erroneously attached to the then Commissioner of the US Patent Office. Regardless of whether it was said seriously or in jest, the consequences for organisations that are unable to find new ways forward are rarely positive.

Organisations who became trapped in traditional thinking such as, 'this is the way we've always done it' have all met the same demise. Kodak, Blockbuster, Toys'R'Us, Ansett, Borders, Nokia, Compaq and General Motors, the list goes on. If the thinking of you or others around you is unable to extend in different directions or ask creative questions, at the very least your progress will stagnate - at worst it will fail. The importance of the intelligent question is well understood in elite sport. A well-framed question is likely to lead to knowledge, innovation and success.

Athletes and teams cannot continue to repeat the exact behaviours of their past if they want to reach the success they aim for. 'The way we've always done it' is an attitude that does not belong on the winners' podium or in organisational arenas. Rugby union team, the Crusaders are a prime example of creative and possibility thinking, and were voted the most successful Australasian sporting franchise of the past 25 years (1993-2018). With consideration to win/loss record, position within competition, stability of the competition and longevity of the club they polled well above other sporting teams, including the Brisbane Broncos (NRL), Geelong Cats (AFL) and Sydney Flames (WNBL).

The Crusaders are a team who have consistently sought to achieve excellence winning nine championships and being runners-up four times. However, their success was not always so evident. In the first season, they lost nine of their 11 matches. In their first game, as a team they averaged 20-30kg lighter than their opposition. Player Mark Hammett described it as, 'boys being pitted up against men'. The team learnt much from that first season, and in addition to the training you might expect from a professional rugby team – video, weights, skills and planning - they also included creative skill sessions, with kicking tennis a favourite game. Not surprisingly the rugby version of tennis is best performed by their regular kickers!

## YOU NEED TO EVOLVE TO STAY AT THE TOP

Sporting teams are constantly faced with having to find new, innovative and better ways of operating and performing. The elation of a grand final win is the pinnacle of participating in a team sport. What emerges the following season is a test of pressure as that team becomes 'the hunted' and every other team in the competition tries to replicate their success. Following the same path and attempting to duplicate the approach in the next year is unlikely to be enough. With your performances constantly under the microscope it is necessary to find an edge, a new approach, change to training or innovative game plan, through thoughtful and creative ways of thinking. The team that is able to continually succeed is the team that can ask the insightful, effective questions and generate creative approaches and solutions.

The pressure in sport is often focused on the journey to the pinnacle, with little consideration to the envious burden of how you sustain the level at the top. In the seasons following a championship or premiership, the coaching staff must refine the strategy, playing roster and the mental and physical preparation. Each of these tasks requires thought and this creative, possibility thinking will be influenced by the questions asked and the answers gained. The better the questions, the deeper the consideration for feedback and improvement to the processes.

Creativity is a foundation to success, because it leads to possibility thinking.

## SO HOW DO YOU ASK A POSSIBILITY QUESTION?

Asking good questions is not instinctive, it's a skill. We can be trained to think more creatively and improve the quality of the questions we ask.

Here's how:

- Start by understanding *what you want to know* – this will include the information you don't currently know (the gaps in your knowledge). For example, I want to know how to improve the communication in my team.
- Then consider *the purpose* behind asking the question. For example, I want to help the team work more effectively, so they get along better and make fewer mistakes.
- What is *the intention* of how this conversation will play out? Do you want an open discussion or do you want to gather facts or opinions?
- How *well stated* is my question? Is it the optimal length - not too long or too short – what I like to call a 'goldilocks' question.

An important insight into improving conversations was identified during a study at Harvard Business School. The research demonstrated that communication is drastically improved when you ask more questions and consequently spend more time listening. If you want to instantly improve all your relationships, the advice is simple. Stop talking. Lead with questions. Listen more. You learn little if you are the only one in the room doing the talking. If you look around and decide you are the smartest person in the room, I would suggest you need to invite more people in!

## HOW QUESTIONS HELP YOU LEARN MORE AND OPEN DOORS

The most powerful question in a conversation is the follow-up question because it aims to deepen the understanding of the original question asked. Follow-up questions are useful because they show the person that you're listening. This deepens your connection with the person and allows you to explore further understanding and intention of the message. Your first question might be, 'Tell me how you think we can improve our performance?' and after they have given their response your follow-up question might be, 'Tell me what leads you to think that is the best solution?'.

Learning to ask better questions will give you more knowledge and information. The better informed you are, the more possibilities are opened for you to explore.

I was once involved in an informal discussion with a soldier about to transition out of the army, and a senior ranked officer. The soldier had served for 20 years and was now considering his options in finding a new career. He made a passing comment about how he had not been a high-performing student at school and said, 'I would have liked to go to university, but I was never smart enough'. The senior officer asked, 'What if you're wrong and you are smart enough?'. You could see the reaction in the soldier's face as he entertained the possibility. Universities have changed. They are no longer the highbrow institutions available only to the privileged, as they had been when that soldier entered the army. We then told him about some of the short courses that were available, the bridging courses, the learning support options for mature aged students. The conversation continued for another half an hour and the soldier left, ready to now explore this new possibility.

In this situation the soldier was too respectful of the rank to initially dismiss the question posed at him by his senior ranking officer. The question though, triggered a whole conversation that included new information, challenges to fixed ideas and motivated him to explore further. I always enjoy the moment in a discussion where the apparent silly question is revealed as an intelligent question in disguise.

## HOW MANY QUESTIONS SHOULD YOU ASK?

The simple answer is, you should ask more questions than you currently do. Did you know that adults ask less than 10% of the questions asked by toddlers each day? Toddlers typically ask 250- 300 questions per day, with around 150 of these questions asked of the primary caregiver. So, if you are a primary caregiver, this is one of the reasons you are so exhausted at the end of each day! Not surprisingly, the least number of questions asked is by teenagers (you won't ask many questions when you are hiding in your cave), with adults typically asking less than 10-30 questions per day.

An explanation for the change in our communication style is that much of our education focuses on supplying and rewarding correct answers rather than a well-considered question. Education also prioritises more time to reading and writing rather than formulating questions. Parenting styles often become more instructional as children grow, also explaining the difference in style through the lifespan. What we do know is that by asking more questions you are demonstrating interest in the person you are speaking to, so in addition to discovering more information you are improving the interpersonal relationship with the other person. With time, asking questions is slowly phased out of our conversations, to our detriment. When you make a conscious effort to ask questions you will learn more, become a better conversationalist and improve your relationships. Asking questions to increase understanding and broaden your possibility thinking is instrumental in your success.

## BE BRAVE AND ASK THE SILLY QUESTION

Next time you're in a discussion pay attention to the types of questions being asked. Notice what kind of answers each question generates and become aware of the patterns that people have in responding to the questions. Create a space that is safe enough to entertain 'the silly question'. A seemingly obvious question might lead to a range of considerations not previously explored. Rarely is a silly question truly silly.

## THE CREATIVE SPACE

Creativity is rarely generated in times of noise, pressure and disruption. Reducing clutter and distractions will enhance opportunities for creativity. You may need to step away from your desk, walk out of your office to find a quiet space, talk to somebody different or make other changes to your environment. Creativity is best developed when you have the right environmental stimulus to generate creative energy. Children are masters of creativity, partly because they haven't yet learnt to feel the criticism of those around them and the notion of success or failure.

## GO FOR A WALK

Good news for those who like a walk - creativity is enhanced by physical activity. This is understood to be a result of endorphin production triggers producing favourable sensations within us, which increases the possibility of new ideas and considerations. A recent study from Stanford University identified a 60% increase in creativity when people combined their thinking with walking. Consider a walking meeting, or if you are contemplating an idea where thinking differently is an important outcome, walk to the water cooler. In fact, keep going – down the corridor, out of the building and around the block. Thinking is enhanced when combined with physical effort.

## TOOLS TO UNCOVER CREATIVE RESPONSES

If you want to ask more creative questions make a habit of recording your observations, thoughts, questions and insights. I prefer an old-fashioned notebook, although concede that these days it may well be an app on your phone. Whichever method you chose, be sure to carry it with you so you are ready to record the ideas and observations that you and others around you make.

Our professional careers often cause us to specialise in a particular field. Athletes are soon required to pick the sport they will pursue, the student studying engineering must decide on their preferred path, the medical specialist has to decide on their chosen field, and perhaps even their preferred body part! This narrowed focus is necessary to develop expertise, however, it can limit us in our ability to think broadly across various topics. To counterbalance our specialisation, our creativity can benefit from opening our interests and possibilities to points of difference. Spend time with people from different professional backgrounds, watch a documentary on a topic that you know nothing about, read a book in a different genre to your typical choice or listen to music from a new artist. Children are curious observers of the world. To a four-year-old, everything is interesting and fascinating. Yet as adults, when we narrow our focus and start to specialise in a particular field, it can be a great inhibitor to the effectiveness of that creative spirit.

A further hesitation people have in relation to creativity is the belief that it is a left-brained arty thing that you either have or you don't. Your mindset here is critical as a fixed belief about your ability to think in such a way will preclude you from the possibilities. To help you move to the mindset that thinking more creatively is within your realms, start small. Think back to breakfast this morning. If you eat the same thing every day, how can you make it different? Could you add a new fruit or different type of yoghurt? Could you sit in a different area in your home to change the experience? We have a few outdoor options at our home and not surprisingly, sitting somewhere different makes me notice new things and opens the possibility to consider my day differently.

Another useful idea is to redefine some of your everyday activities through the lens of creativity. When I worked on research projects at university, I often had the role of taking the dataset and running the analysis. A seemingly straightforward (and not that exciting) task it might seem. It completely changed the experience for me when I considered that the task would enable me to have a world-first insight into the psychology of a group of people. I would be the first to understand how those people thought and how the research variables worked together. On top of this, my ability to collate the spreadsheet and consider the data analysis options would be much better served if I could think of creative ways to view it. This change in focus transformed the experience of me completing a tedious task to becoming the Indiana Jones of the dataset, about to discover new possibilities.

There are countless opportunities in your day to spark your creative thinking. Maybe you could make a change to the chicken curry recipe to give it an unexpected delicious zing? Or change the route for your walk in the morning and explore new terrain in your neighbourhood? All these prompts are examples of activities reframed through the lens of creativity. Treat creativity as a muscle, the more you work it, the better you get at it. Regular reflection of your thinking and behaviour is a great opportunity to explore creativity in your life.

Roger Bannister was a pioneer of creativity. He found a way to reconsider a task that had been done by thousands before him, running four times around a track as fast as they could. His creativity through possibility thinking led to a result that will live forever in the record books.

## HOW CAN YOU ADOPT THE BANNISTER EFFECT TO ACHIEVE YOUR GOALS?

★ Redefine your relationship with creativity. Notice the ways in which you are already creative. What do you do differently to others? Can you identify an opportunity to take on a task in a creative way in the next 24 hours?

★ Be brave enough to ask the 'dumb' question. List five 'what if' questions about a goal you are working towards. Make sure at least two of them are seemingly ridiculous! Find three people and ask the questions out loud. Ask them out loud to yourself and speculate the possibility of the answers.

★ Go for a walk. Whilst out on that walk, ponder a challenge. Consider something you are wondering about. Don't force your thinking too much, let thoughts come in and out of your mind and let them drift.

# CHAPTER 5
# SYSTEMS IN PLACE

> Sports do not build character. They reveal it.
> Heywood Broun

> The secret of your future is hidden in your daily routine.
> Mike Murdock

THERE ARE ATHLETES AT THE OLYMPIC AND INTERNATIONAL level that in their own style and in their own way, always seem to get it right. They are physically prepared and mentally tough. Is this a gift or do athletes have a formula that brings about success on competition day? Whilst the approaches may vary, the patterns of behaviour of many elite performers are predictable. It is almost as if they are following a recipe. A recipe for success.

Usain Bolt, with his characteristic humour and theatrics has brought great entertainment to the start line, and his famous 'to di world' or lightning pose to most finish lines since 2008. In contrast,

Michael Phelps, one of the most successful Olympic athletes is seen pre-competition as quiet, contemplative, often listening to music and centring his focus. Two very different approaches to competition, yet both brutal in their domination of their opposition.

How can such different approaches both work so well in achieving success?

For 25 years I worked as a psychologist. I would often be asked, 'How do you sit and listen to people's problems all day?'. During all my years of practice, it never felt like that was what I was doing. Certainly I met a range of people and would often hear their stories of hardship and challenges. Yet, I've always seen the role of the psychologist as a combination of providing a safe place for someone to tell their story, articulating what would be helpful for the client moving forward, and sharing strategies and techniques that can help them to thrive.

## WHAT IF THERE WAS A FORMULA YOU COULD FOLLOW TO BRING ABOUT SUCCESS?

Within my professional life, my work was under the umbrella of positive psychology. This is a discipline within psychology that considers the science of how to improve life for people so that they can thrive in the world. Rather than work from a deficit model where the focus is on what isn't working, positive psychology seeks out people's strengths and works with those strengths to seek fulfillment. Clients would typically come to my office because they were pursuing strategies to elevate them from doing 'well' to doing 'great' or to get themselves back on track, because something in their life wasn't working.

After a few years of practice, I noticed a pattern for clients who were in the second group. When you asked them to give you some background and to describe how their current challenges compared with better times the script would often follow a similar story:

> 'Well, I used to have everything going pretty well; I was eating ok and getting some sleep, I'd be doing my exercises and I was progressing in my work/sport/study. Now that it's not going well, all of that has fallen away. I've got out of the habit of going to bed early, I'm eating more takeaway and junk, I'm watching too much TV and I'm sleeping in but still feel tired every day. It feels like everything is hard.'

This pattern would be consistent whether the person was an athlete, a business professional or a student. If you quiz most people, they are clear as to what helps life progress well: physical activity, good nutrition, connection with others, sleep, being organised and finding enjoyment in what you do. Yet many people struggle to apply that wisdom daily to their lives. Elite performers understand that the pathway to success is a formula. Once you know the formula the discipline required to be successful becomes instantly easier.

> In every day, there are 1,440 minutes. That means we have 1,440 daily opportunities to make a positive impact.
> Les Brown

To illustrate how effectively a formula works, consider a high-level performer I worked with for several years. The athlete was highly capable in their sport and had already achieved much through their career. After several consistent weeks of high-level performances, they came in to see me. It may seem surprising to have an appointment when things are going well, yet this is actually the very best time to do so.

I told the athlete I was interested in hearing how things were going from their perspective and asked them to reflect on what they were doing in the lead-up to competition; both in the weeks they were competing at their home venue and when they were travelling away. The athlete sat back and started to describe their typical routine. With a notebook in hand I took notes and soon we had a lengthy list filling the page.

The meeting ended, and the athlete returned to training. A few weeks later the athlete contacted me and said the last two performances hadn't been to a standard they were happy with. They described the performances and the unpleasing aspects. I turned their attention to the preparation in the weeks leading in to the two games. I retrieved the page of notes from their file and the athlete was soon moving through my notes ticking and crossing down the list. It soon became clear to the athlete that their routine had changed slightly in the weeks preceding the underperformances. With their routine written in front of them, the athlete could quickly see the small things that were different, which provided an insight into what needed to change. Their comment was, 'I've forgotten how important the little things are'.

The good news is that with the original plan back in place (plus a few further refinements), the athlete returned to their training and preparation and was soon back competing at a high-level. The lessons the athlete uncovered through that session was the importance of:

- having a system in place
- knowing your system
- following your system
- being prepared to adapt and change as needed.

## SO HOW DO YOU DEVELOP YOUR OWN WINNING FORMULA?

Before you try to uncover a formula that works for you it is important to realise that you already have a formula in place. The challenge is understanding what that current formula is and how well it is working for you. Here is a three-step process you can follow:

*Step One:* Decide *why* you want to develop the formula. What will be its purpose? How will you be better for implementing it?

When it makes sense to you and has a purpose, you will be motivated to commit to it.

*Step Two:* Now consider which aspect of your life you are going to focus on. Is it your preparation to start your work day? Is it your stretching and self-care through the week? Is it how you organise your household and get the chores done? Once you have chosen the area of focus you need to take a piece of paper and mentally re-trace your steps, writing down the behaviours, habits and routines that you currently follow.

*Step Three:* Finally, break the formula into the components within the routine. For example, if you are wanting to increase the frequency of using your foam roller for stretching you might:

- have a foam roller in your home (rather than relying on the one at the gym)
- consider where the best place might be to use it
- identify a time that you might use the roller (e.g. the commercial breaks while watching television).

*Bonus Tip:* If this is a new habit you are creating, you can use the steps in Chapter Three to develop a when/then strategy.

Everyone is different and the formula that works for you may not work for others. Within my household, preparing dinner each night is most successfully done, when the meals are planned early in the week. Sunday morning after breakfast is the time that the whiteboard on the fridge is cleaned off and the meals for Sunday to Thursday are written on to the board. With these five dinners planned, the pantry and fridge are then checked so that any missing ingredients are listed for the regular Sunday afternoon grocery shop. The three key steps are, deciding the meals, checking the pantry and doing the grocery shopping. By having this regular inclusion in the week as part of our family's formula we are better set up for our meals for five nights of the week.

Sharing this part of our family formula in a workshop once resulted in a response from a participant along the lines of, 'But how do you know you'll all feel like burritos on Tuesday when it's only Sunday?'. When I invited that person to speak further, she shared that going to the supermarket every day after work was something she looked forward to, particularly considering what her household might like to eat and taking her time to choose the vegetables and ingredients. This clearly illustrates two different formulas at work! The most important part is finding what works best for you, understanding why it works and following your formula.

Earlier in the chapter I mentioned that the best time to attend a session with a psychologist is when things are going well. This is because it is the ideal time to notice and articulate the elements of your formula.

Most elite teams will have a regular team meeting following a competition. One season with a particular team, I recorded the duration of those meetings. Interestingly, and possibly not surprisingly the team meetings following a loss were more than twice the length of the meetings following a win. Upon discussion with the coach we considered the importance of prioritising the elements that had led to the win, as equally if not more important than the losses. As an intervention the coach agreed to lengthen the meetings with the team following a win. This allowed the team to consider in greater depth their successful actions. Whilst athletes will often say they don't like lengthy meetings, my experience is they can actually tolerate them quite well when it's about success. Pay attention to what you're doing well. Be able to clearly state your formula as you can then ensure you are repeating those actions as part of your preparation and planning. Regularly reviewing your formula is a key element on the path to success.

## BUT ISN'T A FORMULA JUST A FORM OF HABIT?

No. The two are different even though they are often spoken of interchangeably. A habit (as discussed in Chapter Three) is a behaviour that is so frequently repeated that it has become nearly or completely involuntary. Our habits are the things we do without needing to give it much thought. In contrast, a formula is a sequence of behaviours that we do often, but not necessarily automatically.

Finding your own winning formula is absolutely essential to achieving your success. With a formula in place, you can free up your thinking to focus on what must be done, then get in and do it.

## HOW CAN YOU DEVELOP AND FOLLOW YOUR FORMULA FOR SUCCESS?

★ Understand what helps you perform well.

★ Conduct your own personal audit that considers all the domains in your life.

★ Write down your formula and find ways to improve on it and follow it.

I have published an interactive journal titled *The Game Plan*. Within it is further content on setting up systems, goals and habits. Scan this QR code to access one of the resources from that book to further support your learning.

www.drjolukins.com/start-stop-more-less

# CHAPTER 6
# TELL IT STRAIGHT

> At the start of each day, I remind myself, my toughest opponent is in the mirror.
> Ryan Lochte

> Always try to associate yourself with and learn as much as you can from those who know more than you do, who do better than you, and who see more clearly than you.
> Dwight Eisenhower

HAVE YOU EVER HAD THAT NIGGLING FEELING AT THE BACK OF your mind, telling you that you're not being truthful with yourself? We often convince ourselves that we really need that new thing we just purchased, that our decision was a good one or that everything is fine (when clearly it isn't). When you don't meet your expectations are you quick to blame others or look outside yourself? How does it feel when you know you are being untruthful?

Humans lie. We do so for many reasons; we want to be right, we want to avoid punishment, we don't want to cause damage (to our reputation, relationship, money or job), we don't want to disappoint others, or we genuinely believe it to be the truth. Whether they be white lies or large whoppers, the lies we tell ourselves will always have consequences. Many of the lies we might tell ourselves are harmful to our wellbeing and may be hurting us in ways we can't see. In professional sport the consequences for lying (to others and ourselves) can be substantial.

Consider these athletes as examples:

- The Spanish Paralympic Basketball team won the gold medal at the 2000 Special Olympics. Described as one of the most outrageous moments in sport, 10 of the players did not meet the qualification of having an IQ below 75. In fact, the players were not tested for intellectual ability to enter the team. The team was stripped of their medal and the associated officials resigned from the sport.
- The winner of the 1980 Boston Marathon for women, was Cuban-born Rosa Ruiz Vivas. She ran a time that would have been the fastest ever in Boston Marathon history, and the third fastest for a woman ever, but was disqualified eight days later. The reason? Ruiz had allegedly caught the subway to the end of the run and joined the course with half a mile to go.
- The 2001 Little League World Series found the performances of junior pitcher, Danny Almonte to be incredible. His ability to throw as hard and accurately as he did was hard to comprehend for a 12-year-old. Sadly, that was because he was actually 14 years of age and his father had falsified his birth certificate.
- And then there are the thousands of athletes who have never attained their personal best due to the stories they

tell themselves. The inability to look in the mirror and be truthful as to the next required step is too painful to see.

When the reward of the prize outweighs the ethical behaviour required to attain it, athletes can travel down a path of deceit and untruthfulness. In a study of athletes who reported using anabolic steroids, 65% agreed they would use a substance even if it would harm their health. Of further concern were the 57% of respondents who agreed they would take it even if it might shorten their life.

Despite these examples, fortunately, most people are honest most of the time. However, the temptation to tell ourselves or others things that are untrue can have significant consequences on our ability to perform at our best. Within the sporting arena, the athlete who is most likely to excel is the one who can consider the feedback and performance data of their training and competition through the lens of honesty.

## HOW HONEST ARE YOU BEING WITH YOURSELF?

How we see ourselves is heavily influenced by the stories we tell ourselves. These stories can be inaccurate and judgmental. We don't always tell ourselves the truth.

When we are honest with ourselves, we can see ourselves more clearly.

Here are some warning signs that may indicate you are lying to yourself:

- you say one thing but feel another
- you're never wrong – whatever it was, it wasn't your fault
- you can't take on board the feedback of others.

The aim of this chapter is not to get caught up in philosophical arguments as to whether truth really exists. However, we know that in any situation there are at least as many 'truths' as there are people. The next time your team loses, turn to the back page or commentary on social media. With a blend of opinion, evidence, and parochialism, the keyboard cowards are quick to offer their 'truth' about the team's performance and other unsolicited advice. What you get is a multitude of differing views, all firmly offered from varying opinions. Honesty, and particularly honest reflection within sport is one of the most useful strategies for improvement. It is also one of the most challenging to execute.

Honesty is not simply telling the truth, but also being real with yourself and others about who you are, what you want and how to be better. Honesty will give you better perception and clarity of your attitudes and behaviours.

The opposite of honesty is deception. Chances are, the times when you've told a lie, you've felt it. Lying is uncomfortable. It hits you at a physical level and you have a degree of insight whilst you do it. The more you lie to yourself, the more familiar you become with the feeling. And eventually, if you continue to regularly lie, you will find it harder to find your way back to a place of truth.

To be honest with yourself, you must get the foundations right. Remember, **just because you believe something, doesn't make it true**. The five key pillars for honesty are:

1. *Trust.* Trust takes time to build, and like a bubble can disappear in a moment. We need to trust those around us, and we need to trust ourselves, particularly in our decision making. If you are reading this as an athlete, or someone wanting to improve within yourself, learning to listen to yourself and trusting your gut reactions and decisions is an important skill on the path to success. If you are reading this as a coach, leader or mentor your ability to build trust with those you lead is critical. This is achieved by being honest in your feedback

and wise in your delivery of that feedback. If those you are responsible for trust your intentions, then you can deliver any sort of feedback, no matter how unpleasant it may be.

2. *Respect*. Respect is a regard for the feelings and wishes of yourself or someone else. Whenever you are engaged in a difficult conversation, one of the key reasons that it may go badly is because people perceive there is a lack of respect. Respect seems to be a fundamental principle and once crossed people feel challenged to engage any further with the other person.

3. *Commitment*. Commitment to an activity is best demonstrated through your behaviour. Commitment is evident through the little things that you do, regularly to help you to reach your end goal. Particularly those things you do when it seems no one is watching. Often commitment is the small things: getting enough sleep, staying hydrated, working through your to-do list, looking after your equipment. This commitment to the little things allows you to know you are being honest in behaving consistently with your goals.

4. *Communication*. Communication, whether it be with others or your internal dialogue is a key element that makes us human. It is also the key reflection of your level of honesty. The way you think matters, and therefore the things you say, out loud and to yourself are some of the biggest influencers on your personal success.

5. *Care*. To care is what makes us human. Compassion and empathy for others is critical in team situations. However, before you can effectively care for others, you need to be able to care for yourself.

The foundations for honesty within yourself and in your relationships are based on these five pillars. When you demonstrate to yourself and others genuine trust, respect, commitment, communication and care, you are well on your way to achieving the basis of honesty.

I have discussed these pillars of honesty at some point with every coach, athlete and team I have worked with, because at all three levels they can be addressed. Those who have the courage to view their own performance and attitude from this perspective are most likely to gain the most insightful information. Some have gone further, basing team discussions around these pillars, and how they might impact upon team dynamics and progress.

## HONESTY AND RESPONSIBILITY FOR OTHERS

Being a coach is a tough gig. You are responsible for the planning of the training, designing and implementing the strategy for the competition and hold ultimate accountability for the success of the athletes. Like the conductor in the orchestra, you are judged on the quality of the performance without playing a single note.

The foundation of the success between athlete and coach lies within their communication. Communicating effectively ensures that an athlete understands their strengths and limitations and has a plan to move forward and improve. Experience tells me that having a relationship that allows for honest communication is critical for success, yet it is not always easily achieved. Effective communication in relationships starts with good intention and effort.

## A PERSONAL STORY IN HONESTY

Early in my career I had the opportunity to attend a workshop, 'Dealing with Difficult People' and the timing couldn't have been better. At that time, I had a client where I felt little progress was being made. The client would come in fortnightly, their recap was literally a repeat of the previous session, we would talk through what they would aim to achieve before the next appointment, they would thank me and leave. The client expressed they appreciated the opportunity to talk, however I was feeling concerned at the apparent lack of progress. To tell the truth I was feeling frustrated by the lack of improvement.

I attended the workshop feeling motivated; surely I would learn some strategies to help get the client moving towards some progress. Soon after the workshop began, we (a room full of psychologists) were asked to sit in groups and role-play being our client talking about us (the practitioners). At first this seemed a strange angle to be taking, however we all launched into the activity, initially enjoying the opportunity to act out through the eyes of the client. We were then told to redirect the focus of the conversation, and now we were to complain about our practitioner; specifically, what annoyed us about them. Here is where things started to get interesting! Sitting in the group our levels of compliance started to waiver. Some struggled to speak negatively about themselves in front of their peers. I decided however that I really wanted a solution to my issue and had nothing to lose. So there, warts and all I complained about myself through the eyes of my client, 'All the sessions feel the same, the format is repetitive, the questions are the same, I answer to the same script and leave for another fortnight no further along than when I originally walked in'. It didn't feel comfortable to say it, yet it was as close as I could get to what might be true for her.

We returned to our seats and waited for the facilitator, but I could anticipate where the focus was turning.

> *"What is it that you are doing that is allowing the client to be difficult?"*

Confrontive, yet effective. It soon became one of my new favourite questions. Of course, the issue wasn't with the client. The client was only difficult and not improving because I had created an environment that didn't allow for it. I didn't need to start by changing the client, I needed to start by changing me.

With my new-found wisdom I returned to the consulting room and redefined the appointment with the client. By changing the way I approached it, the client instantly responded, we made progress far quicker than I could have imagined, and the results were immediate. At that workshop I learnt one of the key secrets to honesty.

In the world of elite athletes, it is very easy to blame others or your circumstances when you aren't getting the progress that you want. This reasoning makes it less likely that you will take responsibility and change your behaviour. Being honest requires strength, so before you look to others as the cause of your problems, first hold up the mirror and look at yourself. Be courageous and ask the question, 'What am I doing that's allowing this to happen?'

## HOW TO HANDLE DIFFICULT FEEDBACK

If the coach (or others) deliver feedback that is difficult to hear, there are several things you should do. The first is to listen carefully. Fight the temptation to talk or defend yourself and just listen. In addition, it's important to determine whether you are hearing a fact or an opinion. While both might be accurate, distinguishing the facts from the opinions will help you to filter the comments and influence your response.

The challenge for you is the same as it is for an elite athlete – to develop the ability to hold the mirror to your reflection and see what is really there. Ask yourself if you are accountable. If things are not working, before you look to anybody else ask first what is your level of contribution to the situation and how might you be a part of the solution moving forward?

Make sure you learn from your poor decisions and honestly reflect to gain insights. Don't waste time harbouring regrets and self-criticism. Instead, consider what you would do differently next time. How can the experience make you better? Self-loathing is a seriously overrated reaction that champions just don't have time for.

To become a better leader and communicator, ask yourself these questions:

- What am I accountable to myself or my team for?
- What is it that I must do better to help myself or them succeed?
- What is it that I have to stop doing?
- How do I really know how well I'm doing?
- Am I receiving honest feedback on my own performance?
- Am I an externaliser? Am I blaming others?

From there, use this checklist to help you find the courage to act:
- ❏ have total commitment
- ❏ utilise quality (rather than quantity) training
- ❏ set clearly defined goals
- ❏ practice imagery on a daily basis
- ❏ focus totally on one moment at a time
- ❏ devote time to your preparation and game plans
- ❏ have a clear understanding of what helps you perform well
- ❏ arm yourself with distraction control strategies
- ❏ give an honest evaluation of your performance.

## WHY BEING 'BRUTALLY HONEST' DOESN'T WORK

Honesty exercises in teams are important but must be well-delivered. I once came into a team to mop up the pieces after an honesty exercise had been used within the group, badly. The commonly used exercise of Start, Stop, Keep had been implemented. This is an exercise where a team sits in a circle with one member 'under the spotlight'. The team member and then their teammates offer feedback as to what that person needs to start doing, stop doing and keep doing in terms of their contribution - and in this case it was, unfortunately, not facilitated well.

With little to no follow-up provided and the 'truth' delivered without due care and consideration, the activity did far more damage to the team dynamics than benefit. The problem with the exercise is that it quickly moves people into thinking about what everyone else in the team is doing wrong. People soon start to externalise and admonish their own responsibility. It is an exercise that I have never delivered to a group, nor would I without hours of individual preparation and follow-up.

There is validity with the term, 'the truth hurts'. That can indeed be true. Whether or not you believe it is warranted for someone to hear it, many people struggle to hear past the brutality of a poorly delivered truth. As a consequence, the person will not grow, and the only thing achieved will be a damaged relationship. Honesty is critical to extend your boundaries and reach your potential. Ensure you contribute to creating a safe environment where honesty can be shared.

## HOW CAN YOU BRING MORE HONESTY TO YOUR LIFE?

★ Apply the five pillars of honesty to yourself and within your relationships.

★ Ask yourself: What do I wish was true? What do I know is true? How can I make it true?

★ Always start with the mirror and consider, what is it that I am doing that is allowing this situation to continue?

# CHAPTER 7
# EMBRACE THE SUCK

> When you're going through hell, keep going.
> Winston Churchill

> Strength does not come from physical capacity. It comes from an indomitable will.
> Mahatma Gandhi

ONE DAY A FARMER'S DONKEY FELL DOWN A WELL. THE ANIMAL cried piteously for hours as the farmer tried to figure out what to do. Finally, he decided the animal was old and the well needed to be covered up anyway, it just wasn't worth retrieving the donkey. So, he invited all his neighbours to come over and help him.

They all grabbed a shovel and began to shovel dirt into the well. At first, the donkey realised what was happening and cried horribly. Then, to everyone's amazement, he quieted down.

After a few shovel loads, the farmer finally looked down the well and was astonished at what he saw.

*With every shovel of dirt that hit his back, the donkey was doing something amazing. He would shake it off and take a step up. As the farmer's neighbours continued to shovel dirt on top of the animal, he would shake it off and take a step up. Pretty soon, everyone was amazed as the donkey stepped up over the edge of the well and trotted off!*

You're tired and exhausted. Your legs are screaming, and your lungs feel like they aren't going to work anymore. You're pushing through the end of what has been a very tough training session. The fatigue may be physical, or the mental effort required to get through a long day or week. A key gap that separates the elite from the ordinary is the ability to push through discomfort when all you want to do is stop.

It's happened to you hasn't it? You've been pushing yourself through a physical or mental task and the self-talk has taken over. You've told yourself it's too hard, or you're too tired, or that you really just don't want to finish it. Then you stop. Then the regret creeps into your thinking. 'I should have...', 'I wish I....', 'Why didn't I just....', or, 'Next time...'.

My work with the Australian Defence Force includes programs supporting soldiers who are seeking excellence in their specialisation or wanting to return from injury to continue their service. Whether they are frontline infantry, on deployment or competing in specialist artillery competition, these soldiers are seeking to develop their own form of excellence. A key session in the program requires the soldiers to learn new strategies to push through physical and mental challenges when their mind is telling them it hurts or it is time to stop.

## ACCEPT THE CHALLENGE AND PUSH ON

Imagine yourself outside on a hot afternoon, lying face down on the grass alongside three others. Within arm's reach is a 40kg pine log.

You and the others beside you must adopt the leopard crawl, a movement where the right arm and left leg move simultaneously followed by the left arm and right leg, whilst your body stays in contact with the ground. With your body low, together you must roll the log 50 metres, then turn around and repeat the process to roll the log back to the starting position.

It's a tough activity. It's physically demanding, biomechanically challenging, and its repetition can cause you to question the point of the exercise, and why the hell you are doing it! Watching the reactions of the soldiers when they hear they are about to do that activity says it all. It's tough and it hurts. During the sessions we first encourage the soldiers to identify their self-talk for such a challenging activity. Its physical demands often (understandably) cause minds to drift to the negative.

*'This is hard.' 'I hate this.'*
*'Will this ever end?'*

Milspeak is used to describe military jargon, originating in the armed forces. Within Milspeak is the phrase, 'the suck'. The suck refers to the discomfort of an activity that is difficult or seemingly pointless. It reminds soldiers that behind every action there is a job to do, and sometimes it simply needs to be done no matter how distasteful.

Learning from the military experience I have taken 'the suck' and emphasised the notion to 'embrace the suck' for athletes. Sometimes the activity 'sucks' because it's repetitive (like shooting 100 baskets after training) and other times it sucks because it's physically demanding (like completing the Chancellor test).

Regardless, the athlete will benefit most from the activity when they are able to embrace the suck.

To embrace the suck is to accept the task at hand. Acceptance is a key requirement in moving forward. I frequently say to people describing distress or unavoidable activities that, 'You don't have to like it, but you do need to accept it'. When we can accept the circumstances in our lives, we are then able to move forward. I am definitely not saying you must like it, be a doormat, or have it overwhelm you. However, you can't move forward unless you accept the circumstances that you are in. Denial, disbelief and rejection, whilst normal reactions to unpleasant circumstances, will not allow you to move forward. They will mentally paralyse you and stop you from growing and improving. When we accept our circumstances, we can stop fighting it and make a plan to move forward.

Athletes need to be able to do the same thing to improve their performance. To reach their potential they must push themselves beyond the point of discomfort into the space where they can become stronger, fitter or mentally tougher.

## ARE YOU GIVING IT YOUR ALL?

Put to the test, many people fall well short of performing to their physical capabilities. But by how much? Well, research advocated by the U.S. Navy SEALs suggest the 40% rule. The 40% rule argues that when you feel like you are completely done with a task, in reality you probably have 40% left to go. Rather than being a scientific rule, the essence is that when you feel like you've reached your limit, you probably have more left, quite a bit more left - and your challenge is to find a way to keep going.

When physically and mentally tested, a person's self-talk is critical. Your self-talk may lift you to the heights of optimal performance or leave you walking away filled with regret. Any endurance activity is ultimately limited by your perception of effort rather than your actual exertion.

I am often asked, why the internal dialogue is so critical. How is it that the way we think impacts so directly on our performance? The general understanding by many of those in psychology is the relationship between our circumstances, our self-talk and our emotional responses directly influences our subsequent behaviour. Essentially, this means that in response to a situation we generate self-talk, and this self-talk then results in an emotional reaction to which we might behaviourally respond.

## IS YOUR SELF-TALK HELPING YOU OR HOLDING YOU BACK?

For the athlete being physically challenged, the self-talk when it starts to 'suck' might be, 'this is what I train for, it will stop hurting as soon as I finish, just get there'. This type of talk boosts motivation and the athlete pushes through and performs well. Alternatively, if in the same situation an athlete thinks, 'I hate this, it's hard, I can't do anymore' then not surprisingly the decline in motivation and feeling of helplessness is likely to result in a drop in performance or stopping the activity. Would it surprise you to know that around 92% of people who start a marathon, finish? That percentage seems surprising to many, but the 40% rule is thought to be part of the reason why so many can push on to get to the finish line.

How easy would it have been for the donkey to give up at the point where its fate seemed evident? The task of escaping the well was not an easy one, but the self-talk was the difference between escape and death. The below example shows how two different people might respond to receiving the same feedback when they haven't performed well at a task:

*Person A*
*Self-talk*: 'I'm hopeless, what's the point? I should have guessed I wouldn't do that well.'
*Emotions*: Disheartened, Worried
*Behaviour*: Gives up and doesn't attempt it again.

*Person B*
*Self-talk*: 'That's disappointing. Well at least now I can see what I need to do to fix it. That feedback will make it better in the long run.'
*Emotions*: Motivated
*Behaviour*: Fix the mistake and approach it with more wisdom next time.

As you can see, it is your self-talk and subsequent emotional responses that drives your helpful or unhelpful behaviours. Day after day, year after year we have been developing our self-talk and our habits of thinking. So much so that we have a common pattern when facing situations in our lives. I refer to it as our default position. For example, when something goes well, you tend to attribute it to your ability. But when things go badly, we usually put it down to external forces or bad luck. However you look at it, our habits are important because we do them on autopilot. We flow into a way of thinking with little internal scrutiny and before we know it, we attain our usual results.

Champions know the habits of thinking and understand that falling into helpful or unhelpful self-talk is the catalyst for your results. To perform to your potential, you need to find a helpful way to talk to yourself. And when things get tough, you need a strategy and approach to push through discomfort and get it done.

## THE IMPORTANCE OF GRIT

To embrace the suck is a reflection of your ability to draw on your personal grit. Grit is the culmination of an individual's perseverance and effort, combined with their passion and determination to achieve a goal. It is a powerful characteristic to have. It will help you achieve an objective and is the foundation for success.

Grit requires courage. Courage reflects your ability to take a risk and manage the fear of failure. When your grit is high you understand that failure isn't the opposite of success, rather a necessary part of it. When we can accept that failure is part of the deal, we can emerge through it with a plan in place.

What will you say to yourself the next time failure occurs? How will you learn from it? And what will you think and do to change the result if you find yourself in that situation again?

## PERFECTION VERSUS EXCELLENCE

Think of a goal that you are currently working towards. Visualise it in your mind. See yourself successfully achieving that goal. What do you see in that visual? Do you imagine it will be perfect?

If so, then you need to rethink that goal.

Perfection is an impossible target. The perfect athlete? The perfect leader? The perfect parent? No. They don't exist. The challenge with setting a goal of perfection is that you set yourself up to fail.

In my experience, perfectionistic thinking has been more indicative of dysfunction than function. Anorexia nervosa, bulimia nervosa and obsessive-compulsive disorder are all psychological disorders strongly rooted in perfectionistic tendencies. Not only does perfectionism set you up for failure, it is a predictor for unhappiness.

So, what then instead? I certainly advocate setting goals that will push and extend you. Goals that are out of reach, but not out of sight.

The key is to strive for *excellence*. I have worked with countless high-performing athletes, teams and coaches. So many of them have been truly excellent at their craft. Not a single person comes to mind however, who could be placed in the category of perfect. That person doesn't exist.

You might argue that some sports lend themselves to perfection. Didn't Nadia Comaneci achieve a perfect 10 in gymnastics in 1976? Yes, in fact she achieved seven of them. My experience is that athletes are the toughest critics of all, and even in a sport where a 10/10 score might be attained, most athletes will still be able to find areas that can be improved or could have been better. Interestingly, the Gymnastic Federation have since changed the scoring to remove the possibility of a perfect score.

What about excellence? Well look no further than the back page of your daily newspaper. Article after article of athletes who can be truly described as excellent at their craft. Excellence is an attitude and behaviour, and derived from the Greek word Arete, which describes superlative ability and superiority. It is the notion that a person is able to reach their full potential. In contrast, perfection was discussed by Aristotle and described as something that had attained its purpose, was complete and was so good that nothing of the kind could be better. That doesn't sound like any person I have ever met.

Excellence is within the reach of all of us. If your goals are viewed within the framework of achieving excellence, it is something you can attain. If you are seeking the perfect outcome, reach for the tissues – because you will be disappointed.

## PERCEIVED EFFORT

Think about the last time you did something requiring physical exertion. Perhaps it was planned exercise, a sport, or you walked up a flight of stairs when the escalator was broken. A critical psychological factor that impacts our performance is our perception of how hard we are working in an activity. Psychologists and exercise physiologists refer to it as our perceived effort. Perceived, because the evaluation of an activity is subjective. If 80,000 people line up in Sydney to participate in the City to Surf Race, the perception as to how hard they have worked will vary dramatically amongst each of them.

What is the impact of perceived effort on an activity? Research tells us that the lower our perceived effort, the easier we think an activity is. Crucially, if an athlete can reduce their perception of how hard a task will be, it will generally have a positive effect on endurance activities. With this knowledge in mind, the opportunity to develop a helpful and powerful strategy is within your reach. Noticing your self-talk through the activity is fundamental. You can then script yourself to be realistic about the effort being asked of you. Telling yourself you are being challenged, but within your capability is helpful - as is telling yourself you can cope with the situation you are in and you have the capacity to deal with it.

When under physical duress it is a common reaction to 'catastrophise' your circumstances. The ability to put the activity into perspective, for example, 'it will stop hurting seconds after I cross the line' is more helpful than overinflating it to, 'this is the worst pain I can imagine'.

## HOW TO RESPOND WHEN IT HURTS

A reasonable question would be, but what about when it does hurt? When I am under fatigue? When I wish it was over? All great questions. Here are some things you can do:

Your first response should be to *check in with your body and notice how it feels*. This strategy is certainly not intended for those who are on the brink of an injury. If you push through to the point that you significantly hurt yourself, you have not listened to your body.

Next, *notice your self-talk*. If it is about the pain and discomfort and it is simply a reaction to the fatigue of the activity, there is a mantra you can adopt. Anyone who has run a marathon knows it is a physically challenging event. Many athletes talk of 'the wall' you hit, in the back end of the race. It's a fatigue zone that you often don't anticipate until you're in it. Your critical response is what you do once you're there.

A mantra that may work for you is to acknowledge the discomfort is actually a positive sign that you have reached the point where the hard work really has to be done. It could be as simple as saying, 'that's the point'. Simple. If there is a part of the training session where you feel uncomfortable, physically taxed, wondering how you will finish the session – that's the point. That's why you did it in the first place. Instead of spinning your wheels thinking how awful it is (which you then feel as physical feedback), shifting your focus to helpful self-talk means you can achieve the target you set when you started the session. Repeating a mantra in a challenging time can be the strategy that keeps you motivated and gets you through.

A soldier in one of my workshops once described a time when he was set the task to run around an oval as a punishment, with no end point identified. He said he had been running for quite some time and was starting to feel fatigued. He said he found a mantra that not only helped him to embrace the suck but made him laugh. He told himself, 'You can't hurt me, I'm a jellyfish'! Over and over he repeated the phrase, helping him to push through the discomfort of the task. I do hope the commanding officer didn't see him laugh! There are so many important reasons why the ability to embrace the suck to push through discomfort and find a new level of possibility is key - in sport, business and in life. It sets you up to learn and grow, is an incredible form of self-discipline and allows you to push through to the next level of achievement.

If you are unable to push through the uncomfortable times, you will give up more easily, not achieve to your potential, and at some level will know that you are not doing what you are capable of. If you are happy with where you are at, then you don't need this skill. If you want to be better, then it's a skill to develop.

This lesson from elite performers transfers to so many aspects of our lives. Whether you are learning to play a new instrument, wanting to get a lengthy project finished, or trying to read a book when reading isn't really 'your thing'. Through our daily lives we encounter activities which are difficult, challenging, onerous, or quite simply, they suck.

So, what will you do at the critical point when your inner voice is telling you to stop? When you understand that to embrace the suck will allow you to push through discomfort, you will have a strategy that helps you to push through and find that 40% the SEALs believe most won't ever achieve.

## HOW CAN YOU STRENGTHEN YOUR RESOLVE TO 'EMBRACE THE SUCK'?

★ Change your words. Stop saying you failed to get the time you wanted, or you failed at your interval session today because your paces were out. Use it as a learning opportunity to see where things went wrong and say that you are learning from your slower times instead of being failed by them.

★ Use challenge as opportunity. Those hills? They're not hard, they're an opportunity for you to get stronger. That interval workout at the track? It's a chance for you to get comfortable with being uncomfortable and see how hard you can push and how much you are capable of.

★ Celebrate your growth. We say running is about just putting one foot in front of the other. And so, every day that you go out and you do more than that and you kick some butt and nail your workout, it's growth. It's progress. And it's worth celebrating. Give yourself a little credit every day, not banking it all up until race day in the hopes that you achieve what you want and get to have the credit. You get to have it now.

★ Cultivate grit. It's that drive, that perseverance, that deep determination, that little part inside of you that comes out when your run sucks and you hurt and it's hard and you keep going anyway. Let that shine! It's moments like that which show you what you are capable of and help you grow.

★ Embrace the suck. If you want to get faster, stronger, better, and go farther, it's not going to be easy. But if you let yourself quit just when it starts getting hard, you also aren't going to get there. When you go out for a hard run, and it sucks and you're in pain and you want to pull back or go home, embrace the suck and keep going. It's the best way to get there. Embrace the discomfort – see it for what it is, an opportunity to be better, to improve, to grow.

★ Value the process (and the time that it takes). Don't be focused only on the end goal, the last step, the big ending. Instead, focus on each step to get there, and appreciate it for being just that: a process that you are progressing through. And remember that good things take time!

# CHAPTER 8
# LIFE BALANCE B.S.

> So there's no such thing as work-life balance. There's work, and there's life, and there's no balance.
>     Sheryl Sandberg

> I don't like the word 'juggling' or 'work-life balance'. You prioritise.
>     Joanna Coles

THERE IS A COST TO BECOMING THE HUMAN EQUIVALENT OF A sports car. When an athlete embarks on the journey of reaching the pinnacle of their sport, the personal investment is substantial. Is 'having it all' a myth? What is it to be completely fulfilled in life? What are you willing to give up?

Donald George Bradman, AC is widely regarded as the greatest batsman to play cricket. His brilliance certainly did not occur through coincidence and the black and white footage of him practising on his Bowral back verandah is well-known. Hour after hour,

Bradman would use a stump to hit a ball rebounding from a cylindrical surface on to uneven ground. Bradman had famously developed his ability to hit and control the ball utilising a water tank, a cricket stump and a golf ball. The degree of difficulty of the task is enormous and his talent for controlling a fast, erratic ball with unpredictable movement should not be underestimated. Repeatedly, Bradman prioritised and endured the hours of deliberate practice needed to develop that one particular skill for his sport.

Research by Swedish psychologist Anders Ericsson and colleagues found that talent is best enhanced by deliberate practice. The amount of practice will vary across endeavours, however acquisition of expertise can be achieved with as few as 4,000 hours of practice. Are you reading this and thinking, 'I'm sure the benchmark is 10,000 hours?' The 10,000-hour rule made famous through the writings of Malcolm Gladwell in his book *Outliers* is often argued as the number of hours of practice required to become world-class. This equates to 20 hours per week over 10 years.

Recent research from Princeton University tells us that deliberate practice is important, but the number of hours needed is variable. Ten thousand hours was the neat number of hours practised by the best violin students, by 20 years of age - and while these students were very good, they were not yet expert. Recipients of prizes in international violin competitions are typically around 30 years old and will generally have 20-25,000 hours of practice under their belts.

So, is practice alone enough? Look back through the last set of notes that you wrote by hand. By 30 years of age it is estimated that you have spent at least 12,000-15,000 hours writing by hand. If the 10,000-hour rule applies and improvement is defined by amount of time invested, then you will be well prepared to take up the art of calligraphy. Admittedly the digital age now leaves us at a point where handwriting is sadly becoming a dying art, as the pen is replaced with the keyboard. However, even with that change, we have all completed enough hours of writing that our progress should be evident. This of course is not the case, with some studies reporting that a third of adults struggle to read their own handwriting. For many of us, the 10,000+ hours invested, have not served us well!

So why has your handwriting not improved over the years? You may conclude it's either not a priority for you or you haven't been taught strategies for improvement. The other reason will be that you haven't spent your time writing consciously thinking about doing it better. The key point here is, that to see real improvement, you need the focus of *deliberate practice*. Deliberate practice is not just completing a task – it is structured, effortful and generally not a whole lot of fun. You need to fully immerse yourself in what you are doing, to achieve the final goal of improvement.

## YOUR TIME, YOUR CHOICE

The lesson from this research is clear – improvement takes time. Thoughtful time. You need to immerse yourself in activities to increase your skill, be well-guided and repeat your efforts and practice as you move towards excellence. Be prepared to invest your most valuable resource – your time. Donald Bradman (wisely it would seem) chose to prioritise the skill of reaction to the ball, and his cricket accomplishments will forever be noted in the halls of history. During this time of developing his expertise, Bradman made an additional choice. The time he spent on his back verandah hitting the ball was not spent on anything else. He could have played piano, spent time with his friends, attended to chores or undertaken study. He didn't. He chose cricket, and specifically reaction time and accuracy over all other things. To specialise in any area of your life is a two-fold choice: what you will make your focus and where you will invest your time. To choose one focus is to forgo attention to other things. This is a choice and all choices will have consequences that you must live with and accept.

Time is your most precious commodity. To excel in any area of your life will take an investment of your time. One choice means the decline of another and you must either forfeit it completely or choose to compromise part of your excellence in that area.

One way to think about your time is as your financial adviser may guide you to consider your money. You have a set amount of money at your disposal. To make a financial investment decision, you would consider those funds that are available for you, the relative risk, and the gains to be had. You can't spend money you don't have. There is a limit to the amount of investments you can make. This is true for your finances and your life commitments. The resources you have to devote across the areas of your life are finite. Expertise in all areas is rarely achieved.

Each week you are given an amount of time at your disposal. From Monday to Sunday you have 168 hours, or if size matters to you, 10,800 minutes. Full stop. That's it. So regardless whether you are a queen or a pauper, your allocation is the same. You don't control time which is why a time management course would be of little value. You don't manage time. You instead, manage yourself through time. The number of years you will live are unknown, the final number of minutes likely out of your control. The importance is that what you do during that time, and what you place priority on is of your choosing. It is important to invest your time thoughtfully and wisely.

## THE MYTH OF A BALANCED LIFE

The truth is, work-life balance is impossible because those things of excellence that you view as worthy of pursuit will cause life to unbalance. You have choices to make. What are the things in your life that you value and want to pursue and what are the things that you are prepared to let go of, either for now or forever? You can make the decision to pursue many things in your life. In which case you will need to develop an acceptance that you will have an imperfect variety of pursuits. Alternatively, you may seek out excellence in particular areas, but you will not achieve this for everything. There is not enough time.

 I hate the term 'work-life balance,' I think it's a setup, and it's a trap for all of us.
    Ruth Porat

The notion that life is a set of scales with one key element on one side and everything else on the other is a fallacy. The idea that these things should be perfectly balanced is both flawed and elusive. As much as we may wish to attain it, a balanced life is unrealistic and unattainable.

Can you have it all? This question is so commonly responded to with a resounding no. I would be more inclined to argue more positively. You can't expect to have it all – at once. The key is to very clearly understand your values and your timing.

Athletes understand this. Sport dependent, the window of opportunity for most athletes is relatively narrow. In the sport of gymnastics, you are generally considering retirement by 20 years of age. In contrast an ultra-distance cyclist peaks at around 39 years. The average age for setting a world record is 26.1 years. Examples of athletes making Olympic teams, such as Dara Torres who swam for the USA at age 41 years are rare exceptions. In fact, only 1.8% of Olympians competing in London 2012 were aged over 40 years. To pursue an athletic endeavour, most athletes need to start in their earlier years.

Your pursuits and the decision to specialise will vary in requirements depending on the nature of the challenge. But here are some tips that will help:

- *Know your purpose* – what are you passionate about? Understand what brings you satisfaction or challenges you.
- *Make better choices* with your behaviours and your timing. Be wise with the scheduling of your time. If you work most effectively in the morning, use this time for your more important projects. This is not the time to be trawling through your social media. If the last thing you do before bed is check your emails, and you don't sleep well, why are you surprised?
- *Consider the consequences* of your choices. If our life is a garden, what we tend to, care for, water and nourish will be the things that grow and flourish. If you ignore a part of your life – your health, partner, family or career, don't be surprised when it wilts.

A story that captures the lessons of balance and timing is The Jar of Rocks. This is a demonstration I used to give in my lectures and would invariably end up in a soggy mess at the front of the theatre. Thankfully there are now videos to make the point much easier!

Large rocks are placed inside a glass jar, right to the top. The audience is asked if the jar is full, the answer is always 'yes'. A bag of gravel is then poured into the jar, around the rocks. The question is repeated, 'Is the jar full?', more nods across the room. A container of sand is poured into the jar, filling the gaps between the gravel and the rocks. Caution across the faces of the audience as the question is repeated again. A pitcher of water (this is where it gets messy!) is poured into the jar and the room can finally agree that the container is full. The students are asked to reflect on the learnings from the exercise. The most typical first response, is 'If you try hard enough you can always fit more in'. An interesting perspective on life! The second consideration is to ask the room whether all those elements would have fitted into the jar if they had been placed in a different order? The key learning here is that prioritising the 'big rocks' in your life is important – or else they will never fit in.

The challenge with the big rocks however is these are the larger, time consuming tasks so often avoided or delayed as they seem too big or too difficult. More often we choose to fill our time with the sand and the gravel.

What are your 'big rocks'? What is your gravel and sand? How well do you fit the big rocks into your jar and how well do you attend to them?

Donald Bradman was clear as to the big rocks in his life. Excellence as a cricketer dominated his life for years. With a clear focus on his goal, the time was prioritised to craft his skill. If you wish to seek excellence in a domain of your life, you need to be clear on how it fits in and find ways to attend to it to reach excellence. You need to understand that not every rock, piece of gravel or grain of sand will fit in your jar.

## IS IT URGENT OR IMPORTANT?

Focus can become misdirected when urgency is confused with importance. With the competing demands in your life, this simple idea can assist you to evaluate how to respond. Tasks and opportunities vary according to their relative level of importance and urgency. Correctly identifying the two elements will help to guide the best course of action.

Think of highly important and urgent tasks as those which were either unforeseen or the result of procrastination. For example, your house is on fire, or your motor vehicle insurance is due at midnight. These tasks require immediate or prompt attention. For those that you've left until the last minute, planning ahead and avoiding procrastination are your strategies to eliminate this challenge. If you feel like you are constantly dealing with important and urgent tasks, you need to review how you schedule your time.

Then there are those tasks that have high importance yet are not urgent. These are likely to be your big rocks. I learnt this the (long) hard way when completing my PhD. For me personally this was an important goal, and one which I was motivated to complete. Keen to finish, but clearly not viewed with sufficient urgency, my lesson was that intention is a great start, however, it is not enough to get something finished. In a university system that did not have a firm deadline, it may be of no surprise that it took me 11 years to complete! Other tasks (the gravel and the sand of my life) would take priority over this goal.

In the end, a key reason I was able to finally complete my thesis was because my two patient (and exasperated) supervisors made it clear to me that my PhD was not their, nor my, life work and it was time to finish it. They helped me set a due date, the new deadline was respected, and I got it completed.

If you ignore the big rocks in your life, one of two things will happen – the urgency will change and it will soon become important and urgent, or the rock will disappear. What would that mean for you? How would you feel if the big rock you identified earlier, was no longer a part of your life? Actively scheduling time into your diary is important to ensure the big rocks receive sufficient attention. The less important tasks that require urgency, often relate to other people. These are the projects or tasks that prevent you from reaching your goals. They are the demands placed upon you, by those who are around you. There is one word that can help in this scenario. It is short and effective yet seemingly difficult for many to say - no. Saying no, encouraging others to solve the problem, or delegating the task to someone else may be appropriate solutions to minimise these distractions in your life. When you say no to a task you are prioritising your own needs and goals. It can be a liberating skill to learn.

Finally, the non-important and non-urgent tasks are your life's distractions. Social media, computer games, binge watching your favourite television series. Most of these are the tasks that really suck your time as they don't contribute to your end goals. To deal with these you need to say no to the requests, delete the games off your phone and be clear about your objectives and boundaries.

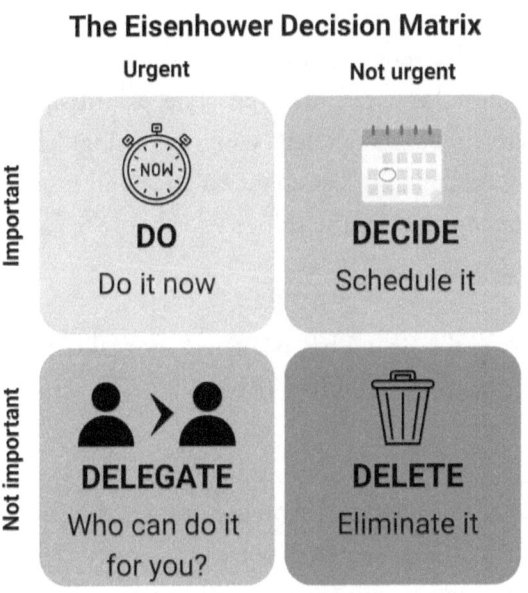

Part of the experience of writing this book occurred at a writer's retreat. There I met a fellow author, and part of our discussion turned to where we invest our time. She confessed that she could probably 'trim' her email inbox because there were too many messages within it. A common confession for many. I asked her what caused her to have too many emails and she said that she finds things interesting, and she would like to go back and read them 'one day'. I asked her how many emails were in her inbox? Ninety thousand. Yes, that is correct – 90,000. She even showed me. I still can't process it and I'm amazed her laptop could even store them! She said the emails had a paralysing effect on her, meaning that she didn't read any of them. Such a great example of unimportant, non-critical information that is so much better sent to the trash.

*The key message to take from this is to understand your relationship with time. What are the elements that are important in your life? How will you prioritise them? And most importantly, what are you choosing to let go of, or not experience at a level of excellence?*

Bradman understood that expertise as a batsman would require a choice about how he spent his time. The prioritising of time spent practising has to be reconciled with the things that will not be attended to. Excellence is less about balance and more about seeking synergy and acceptance of the things you choose to do.

## HOW CAN YOU BETTER MANAGE YOURSELF WITHIN THE DEMANDS OF YOUR LIFE?

★ Take off your busy badge. If you are prone to telling someone you are too busy, try telling them it is not your priority. This is a great strategy for reminding yourself what is important.

★ Know your values and ensure your behaviours are consistent with those values. If you value your health, prioritise activities that enhance your health. If you value your learning, find ways to include learning activities in your life, for example study, watch documentaries, or read more often.

★ Think of the things you do within the categories of the rocks, the gravel or the sand of your life. Use those categories to help you make the choices that are most helpful for you.

★ Ask yourself how an activity fits in terms of importance and urgency. This will also assist you to make choices that allow you to be more in control of your life.

## CHAPTER 9
## IN YOUR CORNER

> You can do anything as long as you have the passion, the drive, the focus and the support.
> Sabrina Bryan

> Just remember: to be grateful and thank the people who are there and support you along the way is a great start to success.
> Meryl Davis

WHEN SHE DECIDED TO TAKE ON AN ULTRA-ENDURANCE RACE she had no idea just how mentally challenging it would be. Her previous distance had been marathons, but a multi-sport event that would take the better part of the day was something she couldn't completely comprehend through her months of training. It was raining, it was cold and after 9 hours she just wanted to stop. She hadn't seen another competitor in the last 20 minutes and the fatigue in her body resonated through her. It felt like even her teeth were tired.

Fighting back tears she reached into her backpack and took out the last thing she had that might help, her mobile phone. At the other end of the phone was the one person who could talk her through her pain and get her going again: her mum.

While the athlete competes on the big stage, there is often a team of family and friends who are watching from the wings. They likely have made a sizeable commitment as well as financial and lifestyle sacrifices so that the athlete might pursue their dreams. Standing on the podium to receive their trophy and deliver their acceptance speech, the athlete will invariably always include an expression of gratitude to those who have contributed to their success. This may include coaches, teammates, health professionals, friends, parents and family. Each of these people make a unique contribution, which plays a role in the performance of the elite athlete throughout their career. This moment reinforces a key principle from the work of positive psychology: people matter.

Research on the formula for success of Olympic athletes includes the expected variables of positivity, motivation, focus and self-confidence. In addition, family and social support throughout the sporting journey is a substantial predictor of sporting success. Interestingly, it seems that the level of social support athletes receive provides not only a feel-good factor but can also directly influence performance. In a study of 200 elite golfers, relative levels of social support systems were explored in addition to confidence levels, stress and anxiety. During high-pressure tournaments, players with strong social support saw improvements in their games by one shot per round of golf. In comparison, those with little social support saw a three shot per round addition to the total score.

A theory which attempts to explain the positive effect of social support on performance is the buffering effect model. It argues that a person's perception of stress is filtered or 'buffered' through their level of social support when they try to understand and cope with stress. In other words, social support influences the negative relationship between stress and our reaction to it. When we feel stressed, knowing we have genuine support makes the experience easier to manage.

## THE FOUR TYPES OF SOCIAL SUPPORT

Support is the network you turn to in times of need. This wise investment in your physical health and mental wellbeing will help you in your ability to cope and your readiness to thrive. Types of support vary, and your personal preference and need will influence the support you seek and the support you offer to others. Let's explore the four key types:

*Tangible support* comes from help with the practicalities of life. It might be the friend who brings you dinner when you are unwell, goes and buys you things when you need them or picks you up when you need a lift.

*Information support* comes from those who can offer advice or information to help you solve a problem. Guidance in how to handle a situation or suggestions for how to be better is helpful for when you are unsure of the next step to take.

*Esteem support* is social support that offers you encouragement and enhances your wellbeing. Esteem support may be the person who points out the strength that you might be neglecting or overlooking or corrects you when you unfairly criticise yourself.

*Emotional support* is the type that involves the physical and emotional comfort associated with empathy and understanding. Whether it be a hug, pat on the back or the gift of listening, emotional support is important for many athletes, particularly in trying times.

In the instance of an injured athlete, they may require all four types of support. They might need someone to help them get to medical appointments, assist with their groceries and cooking their meals, provide advice on the best course of action during recovery and someone to talk to about how upset they are about the injury and ways in which they are struggling emotionally. Each of those needs tap in to the different types of social support that might be available.

The support you need in any given circumstance will vary. Most people have preferences or a default position either to the type of support they crave or the type of support they are most comfortable to give. Think about three key people in your life that you might go to if you had a problem you wanted to share. For each one in turn, think about the type of support they most likely would offer you. Not only does it say much of their default social support style, it will tell you much about what you typically want from others.

With four key different styles of support it is important to understand that the support you *want* in a given situation may not match what is *offered* to you by others. Sometimes the reason why people may feel misunderstood through difficult times is they haven't articulated their needs. Rather than rely on the telepathy of your family, friends, coaches and other support people, tell them what you need. Think carefully about who you seek support from, before you seek it. If you want practical assistance, go to someone who is practical. When you want someone to sit and listen to you without offering advice, go to a friend who does that well. And when you are supporting others, ask them how you can do it best.

## MAKE IT REAL

The coach/athlete relationship is strongly influenced by the level and quality of support developed within it. The type of support coaches offer, the way they deliver feedback and the willingness of athletes to take on board such feedback is critical to the success of the relationship and its impact on performance. A constant comment I hear from athletes is wishing they could get more detail from coaches on how to improve. The feeling is often that the deficits are clearly identified, but the path to improvement isn't always clear. In some teams, athletes may be 'benched' or dropped a grade in the competition and not always understand why, or what they need to do to get back to their original position.

It is important for coaches to ensure their feedback is clear and for athletes to ask their coaches for more information if they don't feel they have enough to help them see the pathway forward. This lesson is important for anyone in a leadership position to consider. If your team members don't understand their strengths, their limitations, and their pathway to improvement then you haven't fully done your job.

I should also point out the challenges with too much positive feedback. It is indeed the case that you can have too much praise. I worked once with an athlete who had previously had a particularly tough coach. The behaviour of the coach included described outbursts and throwing of things around the training facility, which created a culture of fear within the team. The following year the athlete worked with a new coach, and the style couldn't have been more different. Before long the athlete was in my office. 'Jo, I never thought I'd say this, but the coach is too positive'. Is it possible to be too positive? It would seem so. The feedback from the coach was consistently about how well everyone and everything was going. Which sounds great, except from the perspective of the athletes, it wasn't. The feedback didn't seem genuine. The athlete was of the firm opinion that they could break a team rule and the coach would still give them positive feedback.

I can remember years ago one of my sons played in a football carnival where their team was resolutely beaten in every game. It was not pretty. From memory, the 10-0 scoreline was the kindest, and the games only went for 20 minutes! On the sideline was a most enthusiastic parent who genuinely wanted the best for our children. He would give them high-5s, cheer them constantly and tell them how fantastic they were after every game. Most definitely well-intentioned, however the children saw right through it, as was evident in my son's genuine question on the trip home, 'Why are parents allowed to lie? We were terrible.' For feedback to be effective, whether you are an elite athlete or a 6-year-old, it needs to be authentic. If the recipient doesn't trust what you are saying it won't be meaningful.

Can you have too much support? In matrimonial relationships

this can be the case. A research study with married couples looked at informational support. When providing information feels more like unsolicited advice, the effects are worse than if no support was given at all. However, in relationships where esteem support is thought to be genuine, people will happily receive that in high doses! More commonly around 65% of men and 80% of women report feeling they receive too little support from their significant other.

In the world of delivering feedback and offering support the 'goldilocks' principle seems to be a good guide. Not too much, not too little. Make it just right.

## PEOPLE MATTER, IT'S A FACT

One of the most famous studies on human wellbeing and longevity is a Harvard longitudinal study that commenced in 1938. The 268 participants attending Harvard University were followed throughout their lives to gain a better understanding as to the contributing factors to wellness and health. For those few left in the study, now aged into their 90's, their offspring numbering more than 1300 people are continuing to be studied, giving further insight into wellness over the lifespan.

A key finding from the research showed the importance of tending to your relationships as part of your overall health and wellbeing. Social connection and happiness within relationships were a key finding of the research. A further, sobering conclusion is the negative impact that loneliness has on overall wellbeing. Loneliness is as much a threat to our overall longevity as smoking or alcoholism. In the health stakes we can consider social connection a booster and loneliness a poison.

A meta-analysis combines the data of many studies to make broader conclusions about their focus. One such research paper reviewed 148 studies including more than 300,000 participants. This analysis concluded that social connectivity reduced your risk of dying early by 50%. A further consideration of over 70 studies included more than 3.4 million people. It also supported the idea that social isolation and loneliness were linked to a premature death. In each of these large and significant studies the conclusion is simple: people matter.

Elite athletes who are successful have learned that much like the results of the Harvard Study, it is the people in their lives that can make a significant difference to their performances. Importantly it is the athletes who realise this and understand that support can never be a one-way street that will receive the most benefit. Athletes who lose sight of the contribution of others and do not treat it with enough gratitude may soon lose that important support. Athletes need to understand that gratitude is critical to the social support relationship.

## HOW CAN YOU PROVIDE BETTER SUPPORT TO THE PEOPLE IN YOUR LIFE?

One of the key contributors to your relationships with others is effective communication. If you wanted one tip to significantly improve all your relationships it is quite simple. Stop talking, start listening. It was family therapist Moshe Lang who said, 'To be heard is profoundly healing'. The benefits for someone who feels they have been listened to cannot be underestimated. If you are talking with someone and finding the urge to interrupt what they are saying, be patient and wait. Let the person continue talking. You learn very little when you are doing all the talking.

Giving someone your time and listening to their story is one of the most generous things you can do. Listen more, speak less, and ask how you can best support them. This will improve your relationships and your ability to be in someone else's corner.

In a nutshell, having people in your life matters. There are those who have your back, those that support you and those who will hold a mirror up and challenge you when you need it. Knowing you have people who support you is incredibly important. Your ability to be grateful for that gift will enhance those relationships. Further, your ability to support others is an important part of your life experience.

Does asking for help make you weak?

No. Asking others for help and sharing your personal vulnerabilities actually takes great strength. Give your friends and family the benefit of your trust in asking them for help when you need it.

Here's how you can create a strong support system:

*Ask for help.* Trust your friends and family and share the goals and plans you have in place. Let them know where you need assistance and how you would appreciate their help.

*Work with a coach, mentor or trainer.* A good coach is an integral part of your support system. A coach can take responsibility of much of the decision making, the plan, help keep you focused, provide feedback and importantly, invest in you.

*Lead by example.* Your mood is catching. What are you like to be around while you are working on your project? If you are dragging your feet, complaining, or grumble to others, don't be surprised if people don't want to actively support you. Enthusiasm is contagious.

*Support others.* It is much easier to appreciate the generosity of others when you provide that same support. Who can you support? How can you support them?

## HOW CAN YOU GET THE SUPPORT SYSTEMS IN YOUR LIFE WORKING WELL?

★ Reflect on who is in your team, how they support you and the health of the relationship.

★ Your significant people should not have to be mind-readers. If you're thinking, 'If my business partner really knows me and understands me, he/she will work that out and will do the right thing' - let's be clear, mind reading is not a 'thing'. It doesn't exist! It will work better if you say, 'This is what I'm thinking/ feeling and this is how you can help me'. When this goes both ways, your relationships will be significantly improved when you ask rather than assume.

★ Say thank you. Encourage gratitude within your workplace. In addition to focusing on what has gone well, focus on appreciative actions for staff. In customer service people spend more when they feel appreciated. The retention of return customers costs you half of your initial investment. It's a no-brainer. Developing gratitude as part of the culture of your business will positively benefit your bottom line.

★ Remember – people need you and you need them to need you. Whose corner are you in?

# CHAPTER 10
# THE GRATITUDE ATTITUDE

> At least we did not die today, I call that an unqualified success.
> Fear – Inside Out

> I told the players to see the simple act of signing an autograph as our commitment to the fans that we would do our best as their representatives, and that we fully appreciated their great support.
> Todd Blackadder

ATHLETES ARE ALWAYS LOOKING FOR 'THE EDGE', THE SMALL one percenters that will set them apart from their competitors. This could be found in many ways, from increasing strength and periodisation training, to nailing your nutrition and having a great competition plan. All those things can make a considerable difference and investing time and money into improving them can see you stand out from the crowd.

But what if I offered you another strategy that will help to improve your performance? One that requires no financial cost, minimal time and effort, and will also result in an increased level of happiness. Does that sound too good to be true? Incredibly it's not – it's as simple as bringing gratitude into your life. Many athletes have made this link and now you can too.

A body of evidence is growing to show that gratitude can contribute to improving athletic performance. It works on performance by facilitating sleep, reducing stress, boosting self- esteem and increasing life satisfaction. The bottom line is, when you include more gratitude in your life the benefits will flow out like ripples on a pond.

This benefit was highlighted in my work with a team during their pre-training preparation. Their coach encouraged the team to consider the key 'pillars' for which they were to base their behaviours and attitudes throughout the season. One of the pillars identified by the team was gratitude. During team discussions they explored the many ways in which gratitude could be embedded into their culture. They defined it, gave examples of times when it could be utilised and used it as a framework to define what they needed to be doing more of and identify the behaviours they should cease.

With gratitude established as part of the team commitment, they were able to govern their behaviours and attitudes through a lens of appreciation. They could be grateful through a positive attitude and mindset and were appreciative of the experience of playing for the club and in the competition. Their gratitude focused their honesty and was inclusive of the fans, sponsors, staff, coaches and each other. It was evident through the course of that season that the group was tight-knit and supportive of each other. The great trust between the players was strongly influenced by the amount of gratitude they were able to express as part of their training and their appreciation for the crowd after every game, win or loss.

## THE POWER OF WHAT YOU GET TO DO

When people speak of their daily activities, it is often phrased through the things they have to do. 'I *have to* attend this meeting', 'I *have to* reply to my emails', or 'I *have to* speak with this client'. Athletes are no different. 'I *have to* go to training', 'I *have to* go to bed early', or 'I *have to* do my stretches'. It sounds taxing, like it's a lot of effort and there may be moments where it feels difficult. However, the reality is, that athletes are choosing to do their sport and in particular, elite athletes if given the choice, would not do anything else.

'Have to' sounds like an obligation and often it's phrased in a negative way. But what happens if you change your phrasing? What if, instead of thinking of tasks as an obligation enforced upon you, you thought of them from a sense of gratitude and appreciation? This subtle (yet significant) difference is possible when you change the things you have to do to things you get to do.

Perhaps you now...

- *Get to* go to work (versus those who are unemployed).
- *Get to* go to that meeting (to get a job done, make a difference, progress a task).
- *Get to* go to training (versus those who are not physically able to play).
- *Get to* pick up your kids from school (versus those who don't have flexible work hours).
- *Get to* do your study (versus those who don't have the opportunity).
- *Get to* pay that utility bill (rather than living in a country with no access to running water or electricity).

Gratitude can transform common days into thanksgivings, turn routine jobs into joy, and change ordinary opportunities into blessings.
    William Arthur Ward

## GRATITUDE AND HAPPINESS

Gratitude is a moment of reflection which gives you greater clarity. It also helps you redefine failure and disappointment and is very beneficial in cultivating a growth mindset. Did you know that telling someone you appreciate them can increase your own happiness by about 15%? In contrast if you lack gratitude, you'll often be less productive and effective in the things that you do as it is fatiguing.

A key researcher in the area of gratitude is Sonja Lyubomirsky from New York University. She talks of the three key influences on your overall level of happiness: your genetic set point, your circumstances and your intentioned behaviours. She argues that roughly 50% of your general happiness is influenced by your genetics. If you have chosen your parents well (!) then roughly half of your overall happiness is predicted by your family of origin. Around 10% of your happiness is influenced by your personal circumstances. This includes your country of origin, access to medical services, education and other elements that differentiate your circumstances. Finally (and significantly) around 40% of your happiness is determined by your intentional behaviour. Those things that you choose to do or not do that will tip the balance as to your relative level of happiness. Let's be clear. The above figures are rough. However, they are certainly a useful guide and the take home message is that there are things you can do to significantly influence your overall level of happiness. Be kind to others, maintain a sense of personal control, cultivate optimism, connect with others and be grateful for your life and the people in it and you'll be well on your way to tipping the scales favourably.

## THE PURSUIT OF HAPPINESS

The traditional understanding of the relationship between happiness and achievement is fundamentally flawed. The suggestion is that hard work will result in success and once that has been attained, happiness will follow. This thinking is based on the notion that happiness is the end point, the destination that we seek, the consequence of having worked hard. If this thinking were true it would follow that we will be happy when we have got that raise, lost that weight, found our perfect match or bought that car. Yet that is not how people report feeling. The reality is we live in a time where depression and sadness are at an all-time high.

So, what about money – can it buy you happiness? The short answer is money that meets your basic needs will contribute to your happiness. Beyond that, more money will not yield proportionally more happiness. There is an irony that we live in the wealthiest of times, yet as a community are at our most psychologically distressed.

The undeniable messages from the research on happiness and money is that if you base your happiness on the things you own, and the items you buy you will need considerable funds and a large home in which to place them. The 'shelf-life' of happiness from the things we buy is relatively short. You need regular injections of spending if you want to base your happiness on that strategy.

## WHAT ARE THE BENEFITS OF BEING HAPPY?

Seemingly an obvious question, yet it took a large ambitious study to pinpoint the answers. A meta-analysis by Lyubomirsky and colleagues was conducted and it found the following:

Happy people:

- are more productive and more creative
- make more money and have superior jobs
- are better leaders and negotiators
- are more likely to marry and have fulfilling marriages
- are less likely to divorce
- have more friends and social support
- have stronger immune systems, are physically healthier and live longer
- are more helpful and philanthropic
- show more resilience to stress and trauma.

It's clear that happiness has a positive and worthwhile connection with many of the pursuits in life we wish to achieve.

One of my favourite research findings is that happy people live longer. Regardless of personal circumstances, health experiences are improved for those who are happier. When you are happier you are more likely to have better health habits, go to the doctor, exercise, eat well and have a boosted immune system. This gives us ample reason to keep happiness firmly on the radar.

A fascinating study conducted in the United States had healthy participants come in to the laboratory and complete a happiness questionnaire. They were then administered a rhinovirus (the most common form of the cold) via nasal drops. Placed into quarantine for five days in a hotel, the volunteers were subsequently followed for a further four weeks. The research demonstrated that happier participants were less likely to develop a cold, and if they did, it didn't last as long as their less happy counterparts.

## HOW DOES HAPPINESS INFLUENCE THE WORKPLACE?

Mood is contagious and how you feel at work will most certainly affect your performance, your outcomes and the culture within your workplace. Ultimately, the collective happiness of an organisation will also affect its bottom line. One study on the effects of happiness at work had employees complete a happiness measure. Three and a half years later the research team returned to the workplace and asked supervisors to rate the staff across several performance measures. Their research found that happier employees were rated superior on generating useful ideas, having high goals for performance, paying attention to supervisor instructions and feedback, and perceptions as to how well they worked with others. The bottom line is that the way you think matters. Your mood is contagious, so ask yourself when you're at work, at home or out at social occasions, 'Is my mood worth catching?'.

The connections between gratitude and performance are not yet fully understood, however, early signs show it does have a positive impact. This chapter commenced describing the team who embedded gratitude, respect and trust into the fabric of their culture. The team are a great example of how having a conscious appreciation of your circumstances, opportunities and the people in your immediate community can enhance your wellbeing, relationships and outcomes.

## WHAT STEPS CAN YOU PUT IN PLACE TO INCREASE GRATITUDE AND PERFORM BETTER?

★ Keep a journal to record your gratitude reflections. Three times a week, at night before you go to bed, write down the three things that you are grateful for that day.

★ Seek out gratitude in your everyday. Notice moments through your day of the small things for which you're grateful – for example, the great car park you found, the sun shining, the tricky conversation that went well.

★ Give your time generously – remember, it's your most precious commodity.

# CHAPTER 11
# ENJOY THE RIDE

> Just play. Have fun. Enjoy the game.
> Michael Jordan

> Life moves pretty fast. If you don't stop and look around once in a while, you could miss it.
> Ferris Bueller

JOINING THE AUSTRALIAN ARMY IMMEDIATELY AFTER graduating high school, Matt (Willy) Williams started at Kapooka, before completing his training as a Rifleman at Singleton just after his 19th birthday. As a young, fit man in the prime of his life he was ready to serve his country and take on the world. He was then posted in to 7th Brigade in Adelaide where he served for two years until deployed to Afghanistan. He spent nine months in Afghanistan as a Crew Commander, where he found the experiences to be highly challenging and rewarding. His love of travel then began, with a mid-deployment trip to Greece and France for ANZAC day.

Returning to Australia he completed training as a Section Commander. With headaches becoming regular at work his boss required him (literally – he ordered him) to get it checked. Incredibly the headaches were unrelated, but early investigations uncovered a 42x38mm brain tumour. The oncologist told him he had a stage two brain cancer. Willy has just completed 12 months of grueling chemotherapy and now lives wondering in part what the next chapter in his life will bring.

Not one, however, to sit around and wait for anything, Willy has one of the most breathtakingly positive, real and grounded approaches to overcoming adversity in life of anyone I know. 'My cancer has shown me to find happiness in the ability to help others, and to smile, love and laugh no matter what is going on'.

Willy now devotes his time to sharing his story, raising funds for brain cancer research and squeezing as much life in as he can every day. Unlike the athletes I have profiled through these chapters, Willy has not stood on a dais or listened to the national anthem with a bouquet of flowers in hand. He is however, in my opinion one of the toughest, most inspirational people I have met, and he meets all the qualities of the elite that I believe we should be grateful to learn from.

> Your age is what you choose to expose yourself to. I like to think in my 23 years I've seen and experienced already a full lifetime. Everything from here may as well be bonus time.
> Matt Williams

## HOW TO MAKE THE GOOD MOMENTS LAST

Most people have noticed a moment mid-way through an activity when they have appreciated the pleasure of what they are doing. Often referred to as 'savouring' this is the skill we can add to gratitude to turbocharge our satisfaction, happiness and championship thinking. When we savour a moment, it is the gratification that comes from delighting in a moment or experience. A key reason why savouring is so beneficial is that it serves as a memory builder and helps you to recall the experience later on. The ability to recall and re-experience a moment is a quick and powerful intervention to improve wellbeing and motivation. If it was a great experience, why wouldn't you want to experience it more than once?!

Savouring is enhanced when you share the experience with others, particularly the telling of your experience. Research shows it increases your sense of happiness, positively impacts on wellbeing, enhances resilience and reduces stress and self-consciousness. For an elite athlete, the savoured experience helps in goal setting and future planning.

> I have always liked sport and only played or run races for the fun of the thing.
> Jim Thorpe

The bottom line for savouring, is that it's not enough to stop and smell the roses, you should savour the experience too.

## WHAT IF IT SCARES YOU?

I have two sons who are four years apart in age. Like most children they both love roller-coasters and there is always great excitement when we can incorporate a theme park into a family holiday. There was great anticipation one Christmas when my youngest was eight years old and finally tall enough to go on the more exhilarating rides. Having lost paper-scissors-rock with my husband I found myself, first ride of the day lined up in the queue for what is known as 'The Giant Drop'. A 115m tall ride that has passengers sit in an eight-seat floor-less gondola. After a seemingly endless wait at the top of the tower, the gondola is released into a freefall before being stopped by rare-earth magnets. The noise from the ride is loud and the screams from the participants can be heard well throughout the park. Standing in the line I took a moment to watch my son and his anticipation to the ride.

If a team of exercise physiologists tested us both at that moment, I am sure they would have discovered a range of heightened physical responses. Our sympathetic nervous systems would have activated increased heart rate, dilation of pupils, increased oxygen and glucose flow, and a suppression of digestion and the immune system. On paper our reactions may have looked very similar. Two bodies definitely ready to go!

I have noticed my enthusiasm for roller-coasters has waned over time and truth be told I would have much preferred at that moment to be in the line for coffee! There we were. Two people in the same situation, with similar physiological reactions yet psychological experiences that were quite different. A parent who was secretly praying she would live to tell the tale and an eight-year-old who was having the best day of his life!

That welcome distracting thought in the line reminded me of the power of labelling human experiences. Nervousness and excitement are experienced in physiologically similar ways, yet it's our psychological labelling of the experience that can substantially vary.

When Cathy Freeman lined up at the start of the 400m in Sydney she talked of the feeling of butterflies within her stomach. Whilst for many such a feeling may cascade into a series of negative unhelpful thoughts of a nervous reaction, Cathy was able to resist it. When she noticed the butterflies, her interpretation was that she needed the butterflies to line up in formation and her body was now able to race. From the wisdom of world champions (and eight-year-olds) we can learn that perhaps anxiety is sometimes excitement in disguise. Life events will scare you. Most of the challenges worth achieving will take you well out of your comfort zone. More often we will be glad of the risks that we took (regardless of the outcome) and rue the things we did not do. Ultimately, your action will tell you something about yourself, that you did not know before. In most instances, what you know right now is enough to get you started.

## A TALE OF TWO PERSPECTIVES

There was once a businessman who was sitting by the beach in a small Brazilian village. As he sat, he saw a Brazilian fisherman rowing a small boat towards the shore having caught quite few big fish.

The businessman was impressed and asked the fisherman, 'How long does it take you to catch so many fish?'.
The fisherman replied, 'Oh, just a short while'.
'Then why don't you stay longer at sea and catch even more?' The businessman was astonished.
'This is enough to feed my whole family,' the fisherman said.

The businessman then asked, 'So, what do you do for the rest of the day?'.
The fisherman replied, 'Well, I usually wake up early in the morning, go out to sea and catch a few fish, then go back and play with my kids. In the afternoon, I take a nap with my wife, and when evening comes, I join my buddies in the village for a drink — we play guitar, sing and dance throughout the night'.

The businessman offered a suggestion to the fisherman.
'I have a PhD in business management. I could help you to become a more successful person. From now on, you should spend more time at sea and try to catch as many fish as possible. When you have saved enough money, you could buy a bigger boat and catch even more fish. Soon you will be able to afford to buy more boats, set up your own company, your own production plant for canned food and distribution network. By then, you will have moved out of this village and to Sao Paulo, where you can set up HQ to manage your other branches.'

The fisherman continues, 'And after that?'.

*The businessman laughs heartily, 'After that, you can live like a king in your own house, and when the time is right, you can go public and float your shares in the Stock Exchange, and you will be rich'.*
*The fisherman asks, 'And after that?'.*

*The businessman says, 'After that, you can finally retire, you can move to a house by the fishing village, wake up early in the morning, catch a few fish, then return home to play with your kids, have a nice afternoon nap with your wife, and when evening comes, you can join your buddies for a drink, play the guitar, sing and dance throughout the night!'.*

*The fisherman was puzzled, 'Isn't that what I am doing now?'.*

This story was written by Nobel Prize for Literature (1972) winner, Heinrich Boll. It's simplicity as a story does not take from the wisdom of its lessons.

*Be satisfied with what you have.* If you are already happy with what you have, why would you seek to change it? Or if you are not happy with what you have, how can you change it to better serve your goal? The assumption that our happiness lies in the 'next thing' is often a fallacy.

*Be in the moment.* Fail to see and notice what is happening right now and life might just pass you by.

*Share your talents and serve others.* What is your gift? What is your talent? What would it mean for the world for you to share it beyond your immediate circle?

*Live your own life, not someone else's.* The grass is not always greener, and you should be true to yourself and follow your own path.

## WHAT STEPS CAN YOU PUT IN PLACE TO INCREASE GRATITUDE AND PERFORM BETTER?

Rather than end the chapter with my own advice, here's some wisdom from Willy:

> 'Do we matter on the scale of the universe? No. We're little specks of dust floating forever in the vastness and blackness of space. But do we matter on the scale of earth? Yes. Because all we have in the end is each other. In this amazing life with the ability to do anything we want. No matter how long or short, don't let opportunities pass you. Tell people that you love, that you actually love them. We won't be here forever. So, f*ck it, why not wear a smile every day, cry when you need, love each other and give back.'
>
> Matt (Willy) Williams

## CHAPTER 12

## SO IT BEGINS

> The beginning is the most important part of the work.
> Plato

> It is our attitude at the beginning of a difficult task which, more than anything else, will affect its successful outcome.
> William James

IT IS HARD TO IMAGINE AN INSTANCE IN THE MODERN-DAY sporting world where an elite athlete might find themselves, immediately prior to a competition with their shoes missing from their bag!

The story of Jim Thorpe is one of trials, tribulations, adversity, achievements, and a reminder of what is possible when you don't quit. Born as part of the Sac and Fox Tribe, in Oklahoma in 1887, Wa-tho-huck, meaning 'bright path' became more famously known across the world as Jim Thorpe. His versatility as an athlete is unquestioned – competing in the Olympics, as well as professional baseball, basketball and American football.

In 1912 he won Olympic gold medals in pentathlon and

decathlon. Incredibly, to achieve this he finished in first place eight times across 15 events. On the second day of the decathlon competition Thorpe reached into his bag whilst preparing to compete in the high jump, only to find his shoes were missing (their whereabouts were never resolved). A fellow athlete had one smaller size shoe which he borrowed and squeezed into and he found a second shoe in a rubbish bin. The second shoe was larger in size, and so he wore a second pair of socks for a better fit. He competed in the high jump and ran the 110m hurdles in a time that would hold as the fastest for a further 36 years. The following day he competed in pole vault, javelin and the 1500m run. He crossed the line, still wearing the mismatched shoes.

## HOW WELL DO YOU MENTALLY REBOUND WHEN THE UNEXPECTED HAPPENS?

The elite understand they need to do the best they can with what they have. Regardless of their talent or preparation, things can go awry, things can go wrong, adversities happen. The best performing athletes are those that can take an adversity and either deal with it and move on or channel it and turn it into an opportunity. Elite athletes perform best when they can accept who they are, envisage their potential and put steps in place to achieve their goals.

Followers of rugby league will remember this moment in the 2015 NRL Grand Final between the North Queensland Cowboys and Brisbane Broncos. Cowboys co-captain Johnathan Thurston lined up to kick a penalty goal in the closing seconds of the game. The kick would have secured the win for his team. He missed.

In the following seconds the cameras focused in on Johnathan as his eyes looked up to the heavens, his frustration evident, and in his words, 'You don't have to be a lip reader to work out what I said in that moment'. Johnathan's professionalism as an athlete is evident in what happened next. He ran back to his team, they regrouped on the field and took on the Broncos in extra time. Very shortly after, the team capitalised on an error and Johnathan was able to kick a field goal that secured the first ever grand final premiership for the Cowboys.

In a moment of disappointment, the ability to exhale and move to the most helpful mindset is the requirement of an elite performer. The challenge for all of us is not to avoid life's adversities, but rather to have a strategy for when the bumps in the road come along. Certainly, obstacles don't form on the path to get in our way. It is far more helpful to think of the obstacles as part of the path.

Humans generally have a bias and tend to pay more attention to the negative. If you receive 10 pieces of feedback, and only one was a criticism, it's incredible how much weight that one negative can have. With that default tendency in place, most people have to work effortfully towards recognising the positive. To pay attention to the way you are thinking and to find the most helpful way in which to view things is an active process. Jim Thorpe was aware that was what he had to do. A tantrum over lost shoes would serve him no purpose and it would unnecessarily elevate his physiology in a way not conducive to performance. Instead, he was able to take an adversity, think helpfully, find a solution and refocus his thinking. The end results speak for themselves.

## ARE YOU READY TO ACHIEVE EXCELLENCE?

Within this book I have summarised the key skills elite athletes have developed as part of their success. These lessons offer an opportunity for you to implement their thinking habits into your life. It's time now for you to review these lessons and choose which you will apply.

*With a mindset master plan, you can consider what's possible and get excited about the opportunities to be better.*

Elite athletes have a very clear understanding that performance thinking is more beneficial than fixed thinking. Using the word 'yet' in a sentence such as 'I can't do that, yet' explores the possibilities of the future and your own potential. When you are open to continually learning, you will continue to expand your possibilities.

*Success comes from methodically doing the 'what's needed' every day. Putting winning habits in place is the pathway to your success.*

Around 40% of what you do every day is a habit. With helpful habits you free up your mind to be clearer in your thinking. Because willpower is a finite resource you need to use wisely - and the more helpful habits you can implement, the less you will draw on your stores unnecessarily.

*The foundation of motivation is triggered through creativity. Find new ways to excel and do what you do differently.*

Don't be afraid to ask questions and challenge yourself to see things from a different perspective to awaken your creativity. You will learn more and open up new possibilities in all areas of your life.

*Put in place your own systems for success. Understand what helps you to be at your best and implement it.*

An understanding of what helps you to function well is a critical part of your success. Your blueprint or formula is the roadmap that will lead you to the goals you strive for. When you know what helps you to function well, you take a positive and proactive approach to achieving your goals. Map out the elements that help you perform best and ensure you follow them regularly.

*Be honest with yourself. When you hold up the mirror and make an honest assessment, you can get real and experience the results you deserve.*

Much of the truth you seek is in the mirror. When you are honest with yourself you will be much wiser for the information you gain. Don't be afraid to look in the mirror - it's where the answers lie.

*You need to be able to push through the challenges, when it gets tough. Phrase it in a way that gets you comfortable about being uncomfortable.*

Sometimes you just need to get the tough stuff done. It can be uncomfortable, and you may feel like giving up – but remind yourself to get better you need to push through. When you can do this, you are able to embrace what sucks, which smooths the pathway for success.

*Find fulfilment in life when striving for excellence. Understand this won't come through a balanced life.*

Forget about work-life balance – it doesn't exist. Instead, make the choice to devote your energy to achieving excellence in what matters to you. However, be clear that finding the time to practise and become great, may require sacrifices in other areas.

*Your success is based on the people around you and those with whom you rely upon for support.*

People matter. You need to know who is in your corner. Understand why they are there and how they can best help you. Be grateful for their assistance and consider in who's corner you stand.

*Seek happiness through the things that you are grateful for. Appreciate what you have and you'll experience gratitude every day.*

Happiness and satisfaction are best achieved through appreciation and gratitude. A person who can embrace gratitude within their life will appreciate the opportunities as they are presented. Be grateful, savour the moments and use happiness as one of your tools for success.

*And finally, enjoy the ride.*

Life is full of wonderful people, opportunities and experiences. By being mindful of these experiences as we pass through them, we benefit greatly from them. Matt 'Willy' Williams epitomises a life well lived. A life with hope, realism and generosity to give back to others.

Every experience has an ending, yet through every ending comes a new beginning. I wish you well through your journey, Dr. Jo

Thank you for reading **The Elite**.
Your time, investment and commitment to your own performance mean a great deal, and it is a privilege to be part of your journey. I would love to hear your views on The Elite. Your feedback helps me to understand what has resonated, and areas for future writing.

If this book helped you, a short review makes a huge difference. Reviews help other readers discover the book and allow this work to reach and support more people.

**Leave a quick review here:** https://mybook.to/theelite

There are many other ways we can work together, and plenty of additional resources to support your journey.

Please take a look through the following pages to discover additional ways I can support you.

# YOUR *FREE* COPY OF THE ELITE SLEEP GUIDE

So much of your functioning is dependent upon your sleep, the time when you dream, repair your body, rest and process information.

There is no doubt that sleep is our best friend, but it can be also our worst enemy. The quality and quantity of our sleep is where we can improve our fitness, sports performance, decision making and mood.

You need to sleep well, and there's a lot you can do to improve your nights rest.

If your mind and body are crying out for more rest, The Elite Sleep Guide will help you create deeper, more effective sleep.

Claim your free copy of The Elite Sleep Guide at www.drjolukins.com/elite-sleep-guide-lp

# DR. JO LUKINS
## PERFORMANCE & LEADERSHIP EXPERT

I speak on evidence-based performance, resilience, and sustainable excellence for leaders, teams and organisations.

**Learn more about my speaking, books and resources**

SPEAKING ENQUIRIES & RESOURCES

# DR. JO LUKINS
## ABOUT THE AUTHOR

Dr. Jo works with individuals, teams and organisations to help them think and perform at their best. Often described as a psychological Indiana Jones, she loves exploring what drives people and turning those insights into practical, high-performance strategies they can use every day.

With a PhD in psychology and more than 25 years' experience across sport, business and education, Dr. Jo has designed advanced psychological training and performance programs for Australian Defence Force units, including special forces, and has supported elite athletes and high-achieving professionals around the world.

Named an Outstanding Alumni of James Cook University, she is a sought-after speaker and media guest, and the author of books on elite performance, sport psychology, high-performance habits and sporting parents, and what matters most to Dr. Jo is knowing her work makes a real difference in people's lives.

To connect with Dr. Jo, visit drjolukins.com

# YOUR *NEXT* READ WITH DR. JO

**Core Performance Books**

*Deep-dive guides for athletes, parents, referees and anyone serious about high performance*

The Elite
Belief
The Game Plan
In the Grandstands
The Whistle Blower
The Whistle Blower Workbook

**The Quotivation Series**

*Short, sharp quote collections to keep you motivated throughout the year*

Quotes for Athletes
Quotes for Coaches
Quotes for Referees
Quotes for Leaders
Quotes for Business
Quotes for Investors
Quotes for Stoic Leadership
Quotes for Parenting
Quotes for Students

You can explore all of my books and resources at drjolukins.com/books

# FURTHER READING AND REFERENCES

**Two: Mindset Master Plan**

Much has been written of the incredible journey of Michael Jordan. Basketball journalist Roland Lazenby spent nearly 30 years writing about him and in his book, *Michael Jordan: The Life* (2014, Little, Brown & Company) he discusses the highs and lows of Jordan's life both on and off the court.

*Are you not smart enough to solve it ... or have you just not solved it yet?* This TED talk by Carol Dweck is a wonderful summary of her work on mindset. Search: The Power of Believing that You Can Improve. If you'd prefer to read her book I recommend, *Mindset: The New Psychology of Success* (2006, Random House).

**Three: Success On Autopilot**

Cathy Freeman spoke with podcaster Mark Howard on the triumph of winning in Sydney, and how she overcame an uncustomary moment of anxiety several months out. Go to Podcast One, *The Howie Games*: Episode 25.

Peter Gollwitzer was the first to research the effect of intentions on goal planning. This was his first paper on the topic: Gollwitzer,

P. M., & Brandstaetter, V. (1997). Implementation intentions and effective goal pursuit. *Journal of Personality and Social Psychology*, 73, 186-199.

US Navy Admiral William H. McCraven delivered the ten lessons he learnt through his navy training, starting with making your bed every morning. To be reminded why the little things matter google: *University of Texas at Austin 2014 Commencement Address – Admiral William H. McRaven.* Alternatively, ask your mum or your dad. They probably gave you the same advice.

**Four: The Bannister Effect**

To gain further insights on that blustery late spring day in 1954, *Roger Bannister: Twin Tracks* is the autobiography of the first man to run the mile in a number commencing with three. Published by The Robson Press in 2015, it makes for a fascinating read.

The Crusaders have won 9 titles, been finalists 14 times and semi finalists 18 times. The only team to be undefeated for a whole season, they are arguably the worlds most successful domestic professional rugby team. To learn more of their journey visit www.crusaders.co.nz

Communication is drastically improved when you ask more questions. The original research on questions and relationships is by

Huang, Yeomans, Brooks, Minson & Gino (2017). It Doesn't Hurt to Ask: Question-Asking Increases Liking. *Journal of Personality and Social Psychology*, 113(3), 430-452.

Research from Stanford University affirmed the benefits on walking for stimulating creativity. Google *Nilofer Merchant* to watch her TED talk: Got a Meeting? Take a walk.

**Seven: Embrace The Suck**

New recruits soon learn that the Army speaks a different language to any other organisation. Col. Austin Bay compiled a helpful insight into this world in his book: *Embrace the Suck. A Pocket Guide to Milspeak* (2007, Pamphleteer Press).

We are capable of so much more than we think. Entrepreneur Jesse Itzler chronicled his month of living and training with a Navy Seal. To read more about the 40% rule read: *Living with a SEAL: 31 days training with the toughest man on the planet* (2015, Hachette Book Group).

**Eight: Life Balance B.S.**

A wonderful step back in time can be found in the YouTube video: Don Bradman How to Play Cricket – Sound. This video published by British Movietone shows footage from around 1935 of an incredible athlete and true gentleman. He also offers some hints that may improve your cricket game!

An extensive review by Ericsson and colleagues offered a framework for the role of deliberate practice on performance. The article was published in *Psychological Review*, 100(3) 363-406 and titled, The Role of Deliberate Practice in the Acquisition of Expert Performance.

The jar of time is useful to remind us how we choose to spend our time. The story of the sand, rocks and gravel can be found in the video: The Rocks of Time at www.drjolukins.com/resources

**Nine: In Your Corner**

Robert Waldinger is the current director of the Harvard Study of Adult Development. His 2015 TED Talk: *What makes a good life? Lessons from the longest study on happiness* shares three important lessons from the study in addition to advice on building a fulfilling and long life.

Knowing that social support offers a 50% boost in longevity makes a focus on relationships even more important. The research review on more than 300,000 people is detailed in Holt-Lunstad, Smith & Layton (2010) *Social Relationships and Mortality Risk: A Meta- analytic Review*, www.journals.plos.org

### Ten: The Gratitude Attitude

I was fortunate to see Sonja Lyubomirsky present at the *Happiness and Its Causes Conference* in Sydney in 2016. Now you can see her presentation too at www.youtube.com/watch?v=F7JDbP_x8So

The influence of happiness on the common cold is more established than some might think. A short article summarising some of the research in this area is available at the website: www.psychology-today. com under the title, *Happiness and Your Immune System*.

### Eleven: Enjoy The Ride

To listen to more of the wisdom of Matt Williams tune in to the podcast he delivers with Hugo Toovey. Find it on your preferred podcast channel by searching for 25stayalive.

### Twelve: So It Begins

Much has been written of the trials and tribulations of American athlete, Jim Thorpe. One book I have enjoyed is by Steve Sheinkin *Undefeated: Jim Thorpe and the Carlisle Indian School Football Team*, (2017, Roaring Brook Press).

Pushing yourself to your physical limits is not as hard as the battles that some people face every day. Knowing the skills to keep us mentally strong is important for all of us and I'm really glad Dr Jo has written this book. My journey to Race Across America has tested me physically and mentally and I hope you too can learn from the lessons in The Elite. Giddy up!

Al Jefferson, *Race Across America Endurance Athlete*

I appointed Dr. Jo to work as team psychologist with the Townsville Fire in my role as head coach. Working with Jo had a significant positive impact on both the team and myself as a coach. She allowed us to reflect on our capabilities and improve ourselves as players and people. I acknowledge the contribution Dr. Jo made to the team in us reaching four grand finals and being victors in 2015 and 2016. I highly recommend Dr. Jo's professionalism and ability to bring out the best in people.

Chris Lucas, *Head Coach*

Dr. Jo has been a key member of our high-performance staff for the Townsville Fire since 2012, and her impact on our success is immeasurable. She works with our athletes individually building their mental performance strategies, as well as working with the team building our resilience. She has helped me understand how to get the best out of my athletes in high pressure situations, and how to effectively communicate with each of them individually and collectively. I am so excited for this book!

Claudia Brassard, *Olympian & Head Coach*

Dr. Jo is great at helping athletes prepare for their mental game and manage the balance of professional sport and life. Actually, she is better than Lego – you should go and see her!

Johnathan Thurston, *Australian Rugby League Legend*

Dr. Jo's ability to convey complex theories in an easy to understand way is a rare gift and I have seen firsthand the life-changing affect it can have on people. This is a book everyone should read.

    Daina Clark, *Destination Adventure*

Very excited to read this book and see Dr. Jo's breadth of knowledge distilled in one place. Jo has spent a lot of time working with the best across all domains, and it shows in her work. If you care about operating at your highest potential, listen to what Jo has to say!

    Dallas Davison, *Financial Adviser & Amateur MMA Fighter*

I've been working with Dr. Jo for many years in the management of a number of athletes that I coach. Performance at the peak of your capacity, no matter what that capacity is, requires a dedicated, focused and disciplined approach. Dr. Jo has an intuitive sense of reading a situation and through this, working with individuals to equip them with the tools to bring out the best in themselves. No matter your goals, Dr. Jo has strategies to enable you to achieve them.

    Dr Deborah Latouf, *Spin Doctor Coaching*

Jo and I have grown, learnt and laughed a lot as we travelled through our professional lives together. This book is the culmination of Jo's curiosity, passion, wisdom and keen eye for translating the science of performance into concepts we can all learn from and apply. Many, including myself, have experienced light-bulb moments with Jo, that led to small or large changes in the way we live our lives for the better. The Elite shares those moments of learning with a larger audience, who can now benefit from Jo's years of honing her skill and knowledge in supporting people to be the best they can be.

    Renee McAllister, *Psychologist*

As captain of a national sporting team the Townsville Crocodiles for five years, and a husband, father and community icon, the pressure can be unrelenting. Knowing that Dr. Jo is only a text message or phone call away is like having your own personal bulletproof vest. She makes you feel like nothing can hurt you and everything will be great. Following a serious injury, I managed to play two more great years in the NBL. Dr. Jo is every bit as responsible for any successes I was able to have as the coach was.

    Russell Hinder, *Captain: NBL Crocodiles*

So excited that someone of Dr Jo's quality and experience has written this book. Dr. Jo has an innate ability to understand people and bring out their best. I was privileged to see the difference she made working with our servicemen and women in Townsville and would regularly take the opportunity to sit in on her lectures to enhance my own life and develop my leadership skill set. This book is full of lessons and anecdotes that will make a significant impact on those who read it.

    Simon O'Regan, *Army Officer: Australian Defence Force*

I have been a professional athlete for over 22 years and have represented Australia at three Olympic Games. After playing at an elite level in all major basketball leagues across the globe, I would count Dr Jo Lukins as a true leader in her field and am grateful for her insight and contribution to myself and the Townsville Fire program both on and off the court.

    Suzy Batkovic, *Olympian & Australian Basketball Legend*

I have been so very fortunate to have worked with Dr Jo during my time as an assistant coach with the Townsville Crocodiles. Dr. Jo made a major impact on my professional life, by working with me on strategies to enhance my decision-making and tactical manoeuvring within the stressful environment of professional basketball. Dr. Jo is not just a leader in her field, but she is extremely thoughtful, engaging and practical with her advice. I can't wait to dig in to her new book, and I would urge coaches of all sports and levels to do the same!

    Liam Flynn, *Professional Basketball Coach*

www.ingramcontent.com/pod-product-compliance
Lightning Source LLC
Chambersburg PA
CBHW031253290426
44109CB00012B/567